Dyke and Carlisle

The Acts and Resolutions Adopted at the 1st Session

of the 12th General Assembly of Florida

Dyke and Carlisle

The Acts and Resolutions Adopted at the 1st Session
of the 12th General Assembly of Florida

ISBN/EAN: 9783337184599

Printed in Europe, USA, Canada, Australia, Japan

Cover: Foto ©Thomas Meinert / pixelio.de

More available books at **www.hansebooks.com**

THE

ACTS AND RESOLUTIONS

ADOPTED AT THE 1st SESSION

OF THE

12TH GENERAL ASSEMBLY OF FLORIDA,

**Begun and Held at the Capitol, in the City of Talla-
hassee, on Monday, November 17, 1862.**

————— ◆•••◆ —————

PUBLISHED BY AUTHORITY OF LAW,

UNDER THE DIRECTION OF THE ATTORNEY GENERAL.

————— ◆•••◆ —————

Tallahassee:

OFFICE OF THE FLORIDIAN & JOURNAL.

PRINTED BY DYKE & CARLISLE.

1862.

TITLES

OF

ACTS AND RESOLUTIONS

PASSED AT THE

First Session of the Twelfth General Assembly

OF THE

STATE OF FLORIDA,

1862.

An act to authorize the Executors of James Abercrombie, Sr., to sell property in certain cases.

An act to allow officers of incorporated companies to hold their offices until their successors are elected, where such elections cannot be held on account of the war.

An act to authorize the removal of slaves and other property from this State.

An act requiring annual reports from Board of Trustees of Internal Improvement Fund.

An act for the relief of Richard Saunders, Sheriff of Leon county.

An act to amend an act concerning wills, letters testamentary and letters of administration, and the duties of Executors, Administrators and Guardians.

An act to authorize the Judge of the Circuit Court of Duval county, to hold the sessions of Court at Baldwin.

An act to authorize the Circuit Courts of this State to change the names of persons residing therein.

An act to consolidate the office of Sheriff, Tax Assessor and Collector of Calhoun county.

An act for the relief of Jailors in the several counties in this State.

An act in relation to the qualification of Judges.

An act to amend an act to provide for the establishment of two Seminaries of Learning, approved January 24, 1851.

An act to relieve certain persons from a poll or capitation tax, and also certain portions of their property from taxation.

An act to organize the county of Brevard.

An act to change the time of holding the regular terms of the Commissioners' Courts of Washington and Holmes counties.

An act for the relief of J. J. Ward, Sheriff of Lafayette county.

RESOLUTIONS.

LAWS OF THE STATE OF FLORIDA,

PASSED AT THE

First Session of the Twelfth General Assembly, 1862.

JOHN MILTON, Governor. F. L. VILLEPIGUE, Secretary of State. WALTER GWYNN, Comptroller of Public Accounts. C. H. AUSTIN, Treasurer. J. B. GALBRAITH, Attorney General. E. J. VANN, President of the Senate. E. J JUDAH, Secretary of the Senate. T. J. EPPES, Speaker of the House. T. B. BAREFOOT, Clerk of the House.

CHAPTER 1,317—[No. 1.]

AN ACT authorizing the Executors of James Abercrombie, senior, to sell property in certain cases.

SECTION 1. *Be it enacted by the Senate and House of Representatives of the State of Florida in General Assembly convened,* That the legal representatives of James Abercrombie, Sr., deceased, late of Escambia county, be and they are hereby authorized to sell, in any of the Confederate States of America, under the authority and by the direction of the Probate Court of Escambia county, any part or all of the property, both real and personal, belonging to the estate of said decedant, which, by the last will and testament of said James Abercrombie, Sr., his executors were authorized to sell, and to distribute the same in accordance with the requirements of the said last will and testament.

Legal representatives authorized to sell.

Property to be sold.

Passed the House of Representatives November 24, 1862. Passed the Senate November 24, 1862. Approved by the Governor November 26, 1862.

LAWS OF FLORIDA.

9

1862.

CHAPTER 1,318—[No. 2.]

AN ACT to allow officers of Incorporated Companies to hold their offices until their successors are elected, when such elections cannot be held on account of the war.

SECTION 1. *Be it enacted by the Senate and House of Representatives of the State of Florida in General Assembly convened*, That whenever any Insurance Company in this State has had to remove their office from any evacuated city in this State, or on account of the war, and shall not have held their annual election for officers on said account, or on account of the absence of the Stockholders on account of the war, said Charters shall not be violated or void on account of said failure to elect, but said officers shall continue in office until their successors shall be hereafter elected, and the present Presidents, Secretaries, Officers and Directors shall continue to serve until a new election shall be had in their respective Companies. *(Insurance Companies. Charters not made void by failure to elect officers. Officers to continue.)*

SEC. 2. *Be it further enacted*, That the provisions of this Act shall be applicable to all incorporated companies in this State which are placed in circumstances like those mentioned in the first section of this Act. *(Other incorporated Companies.)*

Passed the Senate November 24, 1862. Passed the House of Representatives November 26, 1862. Approved by the Governor November 27, 1862.

CHAPTER 1,319—[No. 3.]

AN ACT to authorize the removal of slaves and other property from the State.

SECTION 1. *Be it enacted by the Senate and House of Representatives of the State of Florida in General Assembly convened*, That from and after the passage of this Act, it shall be lawful for all Executors, Administrators, Trustees and Guardians to remove from this State to places of safety, anywhere in the Confederate States, all negroes, mules, horses, cattle and other moveable perishable property, under their control, by virtue of their fiduciary capacity, whenever their counties are invaded by the enemy, and by which invasion such property is rendered insecure. *(Execut'rs, Trustees, &c., authorized to remove property from invasion.)*

Passed the Senate November 24, 1862. Passed the House of Representatives November 25, 1862. Approved by the Governor November 28, 1862.

2

CHAPTER 1,320—[No. 4.]

AN ACT requiring annual reports from Board of Trustees of Internal Improvement Fund.

SECTION 1. *Be it enacted by the Senate and House of Representatives of the State of Florida in General Assembly convened,* That the Board of Trustees of the Internal Improvement Fund be and they are hereby required to report annually to the General Assembly of the State of Florida upon the several matters committed to their charge, and such other matters as may be deemed proper in connexion therewith.

SEC. 2. *Be it further enacted,* That all laws inconsistent with the provisions of this Act be and the same are hereby repealed.

Passed the House of Representatives November 24, 1862. Passed the Senate November 26, 1862. Approved by the Governor December 1, 1862.

Marginal notes: Board of Trustees Int. Imp. Fund to report annually. Repealed.

CHAPTER 1,321—[No. 5.]

AN ACT for the relief of Richard Saunders, Sheriff of Leon county.

SECTION 1. *Be it enacted by the Senate and House of Representatives of the State of Florida in General Assembly convened,* That the Comptroller of Public Accounts be and he is hereby authorized and required to issue his warrant for the sum of two hundred and five 63-100 dollars, being the amount over paid by Richard Saunders, Sheriff, in settlement of his accounts; and that the Treasurer be required to pay the same out of any money not otherwise appropriated.

Passed the Senate November 24, 1862. Passed the House of Representatives November 27, 1862. Approved by the Governor December 1, 1862.

Marginal note: Comptroller to issue Warrant for am't over-paid.

CHAPTER 1,322—[No. 6.]

AN ACT to amend an act concerning Wills, Letters Testamentary and Letters of Administration, and the duties of Executors, Administrators and Guardians.

SECTION 1. *Be it enacted by the Senate and House of Representatives of the State of Florida in General Assembly convened,* That so much of the 35th Section of the Act, of which this is an amendment, as directs the loan of any moneys by Executors, Administrators and Guardians upon Mortgage Security only, be so modified as to authorize said parties and all other persons holding money in a fiduciary capacity, and authorized to loan the same, to invest the said funds in Bonds of the "Confederate States" or Bonds issued by the State of Florida, (but not Internal Improvement Bonds, Seminary, Canal, Railroad Bonds, or any other Bonds issued to aid Corporations,) bearing an annual interest.

Executors, &c., may invest in Bonds of Confederate States or State of Fla.

SEC. 2. *Be it further enacted,* That so much of the before recited section as directs the taking of a new bond or obligation annually be repealed ; *Provided,* that this repeal shall not operate to prevent the collection of the interest annually, and its re-investment as contemplated in the said section.

Annual Bond or obligation.

Interest.

Passed the Senate November 21, 1862. Passed the House of Representatives November 28, 1862. Approved by the Governor December 2, 1862.

CHAPTER 1,323—[No. 7.]

AN ACT to authorize the Judge of the Circuit Court for Duval county to hold the Sessions of Court at Baldwin.

SECTION 1. *Be it enacted by the Senate and House of Representatives of the State of Florida in General Assembly convened,* That the Judge of the Circuit Court for Duval county be authorized to hold the sessions of said Court at Baldwin during the continuance of the war, and that the Clerk of said Court be and he is hereby required to reside at Baldwin, in said county, or to have a deputy to represent him there during the continuance of the war as aforesaid, and that the business of said Circuit Court be transacted in all respects at Baldwin instead of Jacksonville, as heretofore, until such time as said Judge shall deem it safe to resume the holding of said Court at Jacksonville.

Judge may hold Court at Baldwin.

Clerk.

SEC. 2. *Be it further enacted,* That the Judge of Probate for Duval county be also required to keep his office and to transact the Probate business of said county at Baldwin instead of Jacksonville, until such time as it may be safe, as aforesaid, to return to Jacksonville.

Judge of Probate required to keep his office at Baldwin.

Passed the House of Representatives November 28, 1862. Passed the Senate November 29, 1862. Approved by the Governor December 3, 1862.

CHAPTER 1,324—[No. 8.]

AN ACT to authorize the Circuit Courts of this State to change the names of persons residing therein.

SECTION. 1. *Be it enacted by the Senate and House of Representatives of the State of Florida in General Assembly convened,* That the Circuit Courts of this State shall have the power and authority to change the names of persons residing in said State, upon a petition filed by such person in any of the Circuits of the State; that such petition shall state the name of the petitioner, and the name such petitioner desires to take; and the said Court shall, at the first term thereof, decree that the petitioner's name be changed to the name which said petitioner desires, by which the said petitioner shall ever thereafter be known.

SEC. 2. *Be it further enacted,* That all other Acts and parts of Acts in relation to this subject, be and the same are hereby repealed.

Circuit Courts may change the names of persons.

Repeal.

Passed the House of Representatives November 27, 1862. *Passed the Senate December 1, 1862. Approved December 3, 1862.

CHAPTER 1,325—[No. 9.]

AN ACT to consolidate the offices of Sheriff, Tax Assessor and Collector of Calhoun county.

SECTION 1. *Be it enacted by the Senate and House of Representatives of the State of Florida in General Assembly convened,* That the offices of Sheriff, Tax Assessor and Collector of the county of Calhoun, be and they are hereby consolidated, and the Sheriff shall perform all the duties of said offices, and shall give a bond for the faithful performance of the several duties of said offices; *Provided, however,* that this Act shall not go into operation until the term of office of the present Tax Assessor and Collector has expired.

Offices consolidated.

Proviso.

Passed the House of Representatives November 28, 1862. Passed the Senate November 29, 1862. Approved by the Governor December 3, 1862.

CHAPTER 1,326—[No. 10.]

AN ACT for the relief of Jailors in the several counties in this State.

SECTION 1. *Be it enacted by the Senate and House of Representatives of the State of Florida in General Assembly convened,*

That the Jailors in the several counties in this State, from and after the passage of this Act, shall be entitled to charge and receive the sum of seventy-five cents per day for keeping and providing for prisoners, runaway slaves, or slaves taken under execution or other process, or other persons confined in jail under legal process.

Jailor's fees.

Sec. 2. *Be it further enacted,* That all laws and parts of laws militating against this Act be and the same are hereby repealed.

Repeal.

Passed the House of Representatives November 25, 1862. Passed the Senate November 29, 1862. Approved by the Governor December 3, 1862.

CHAPTER 1,327—[No. 11.]

AN ACT in relation to the qualification of Judges.

SECTION 1. *Be it enacted by the Senate and House of Representatives of the State of Florida in General Assembly convened,* That no Judge of any Court or Justice of the Peace shall sit or preside in any cause to which he is a party, or in which he is interested, or in which he would be excluded from being a juror by reason of interest, consanguinity, or affinity to either of the parties; nor shall he entertain any motion in the cause other than to have the same tried by a competent tribunal.

Judges or Justice's of the Peace may not preside in certain cases.

Sec. 2. *Be it further enacted,* That the Judge or Justice so incompetent shall retire of his own motion, and without waiting for an application to that effect; that any and all judgments, decrees and orders, made by a Judge or Judges so incompetent, shall be of no force or validity, and are hereby declared to be null and void, except an order for the trial of the cause as hereinbefore provided.

Judge shall retire of his own motion.

Judgments rendered by incompetent tribunals void.

Passed the Senate November 26, 1862. Passed the House of Representatives December 3, 1862. Approved by the Governor December 4, 1862.

CHAPTER 1,328—[No. 12.]

AN ACT to amend an Act to provide for the establishment of two Seminaries of Learning, approved January 24th, 1861.

SECTION 1. *Be it enacted by the Senate and House of Representatives of the State of Florida in General Assembly convened,*

Governor shall appoint members of Board of Education.

County Superintendant.

That there shall be appointed by the Governor, by and with the advice and consent of the Senate, six persons for each of the two Seminaries of Learning, as members of a Board of Education, who shall hold their office for two years. The county Superintendent of the county in which the Seminary is situated shall, by virtue of his office, be a member of the Board, and shall act as Secretary thereof, and keep an accurate and detailed account of their doings. Vacancies in the Board shall be filled in the manner now provided by law.

SEC. 2. *Be it further enacted*, That so much of the third section of an Act entitled an Act to provide for the establishment of two Seminaries of Learning, approved the twenty-fourth day of January, 1851, as conflicts with the provisions of this Act, be and the same is hereby repealed.

Repeal.

Passed the House of Representatives November 28, 1862. Passed the Senate December 4, 1862. Approved by the Governor December 6, 1862.

CHAPTER 1,329—[No. 13.]

AN ACT to relieve certain persons from a Poll or Capitation Tax, and also a certain portion of their property from Taxation.

SECTION 1. *Be it enacted by the Senate and House of Representatives of the State of Florida in General Assembly convened*, That no citizen of this State who has been mustered into the military service of the Confederate States as a private for three years or the war, and who is still in said service, shall be required to pay a poll or capitation tax.

Citizens in military service.

SEC. 2. *Be it further enacted*, That property belonging to each and every person designated in the foregoing section to the amount of one thousand dollars in value shall at his option be exempt from taxation.

Property of persons in service.

SEC. 3. *Be it further enacted*, That this act shall continue in force during the existence of the present war, and no longer, and that all laws and parts of laws inconsistent therewith are hereby suspended for the same period.

Limitation of Act.

Passed the House of Representatives November 27, 1862. Passed the Senate December 4, 1862. Approved December 6, 1862.

CHAPTER 1,330—[No. 14.]

AN ACT to organize the County of Brevard.

SECTION 1. *Be it enacted by the Senate and House of Representatives of the State of Florida in General Assembly convened,*

'That for the purpose of a more efficient organization of the county of Brevard, there shall be an election held at the different precincts in said county, according to the election laws of this State, on the first Monday in March next, for a Judge of Probate, four County Commissioners, a Clerk of the Circuit Court and a Sheriff of said county, who shall hold their offices until the regular election in eighteen hundred and sixty-five.

SEC. 2. *Be it further enacted,* That the Judge of Probate or acting Judge of Probate of Orange county be, and he is hereby required to give notice of said election in Brevard county, and to appoint the Inspectors of said election, and he shall receive the returns and canvass the same in all respects as if the said election had been held in his own proper county of Orange, and the said Judge of Probate of Orange county shall certify the result to the Secretary of State as required by law, who shall issue commissions accordingly.

Judge of Pro-
bate of Orange
county required
to give notice of
elections, &c.

SEC. 3. *Be it further enacted,* That in case the citizens of Brevard county shall fail to hold said election at the time and in the manner prescribed in this Act, or the officers elected shall refuse to qualify or serve, then, in that event, all judicial and executive functions which should be discharged by the county officers of the said county of Brevard shall appertain to and become the functions and duty of the Judicial and Executive officers of the county of Orange, who shall discharge all the duties appertaining to their respective offices in the said county of Brevard in the same manner as they would and should do in their own proper county of Orange, and the Tax Assessor and Collector of Orange county shall assess and collect taxes in the county of Brevard, and be the Tax Assessor and Collector for the same until said county is organized and shall elect its proper officers.

In case of fail-
ure of election.
&c.

County officers
of Orange Co.

SEC. 4. *Be it further enacted,* That at the time for the election of officers as above specified, there shall also be held an election for a county site for said county of Brevard, under the same rules and regulations as specified for the other elections, and the result of said election shall be certified in like manner, and the place or locality which shall receive the largest number of votes shall be the county site of said county of Brevard.

County site.

Passed the House of Representatives November 28, 1862. Passed the Senate December 4th, 1862. Approved by the Governor December 6, 1862.

CHAPTER 1,331—[No. 15.]

AN ACT to change the time of holding the regular terms of the Commissioner's Courts of Washington and Holmes counties.

SECTION 1. *Be it enacted by the Senate and House of Representatives of the State of Florida in General Assembly con-*

1862.

Terms of Commissioners Courts.

vened, That from and after the passage of this act, the regular terms of the Commissioner's Courts of Washington and Holmes counties shall be held at the County Site in their respective counties on the second Monday in February and the first Monday in November in each year.

SEC. 2. *Be it further enacted,* That all laws and parts of laws, so far as they conflict with the provisions of this act, be and the same are hereby repealed.

Repeal.

Passed the House of Representatives December 1, 1862. Passed the Senate December 4, 1862. Approved by the Governor December 6, 1862.

CHAPTER 1,332—[No. 16.]

AN ACT for the relief of J. J. Ward, Sheriff of Lafayette County.

Preamble.

WHEREAS, at a Fall Term of the Circuit Court for the Suwannee Circuit, held in and for the county of Lafayette, A. D. 1860, certain fines were imposed upon certain parties by the presiding Judge, amounting in the aggregate to the sum of one hundred and fifty dollars; AND WHEREAS, said fines were remitted by said Judge at the term of the Court, next thereafter held in said county; AND WHEREAS, before said fines were remitted, J. J. Ward, the Sheriff of said county, had paid the said sum of one hundred and fifty dollars into the Treasury of the State:

SECTION 1. *Be it enacted by the Senate and House of Representatives of the State of Florida in General Assembly convened,* That the Comptroller of the State be and he is hereby authorized to issue his Warrant upon the Treasury of the State for the sum of one hundred and fifty dollars in favor of J. J. Ward, to be paid out of any moneys in the Treasury not otherwise appropriated.

Comptroller to issue Warrant.

Passed the House of Representatives December 1, 1862. Passed the Senate December 4, 1862. Approved by the Governor December 6, 1862.

CHAPTER 1,333—[No. 17.]

AN ACT to amend an Act for the relief of William H. Fannin.

Preamble.

WHEREAS, the General Assembly of the State of Florida, at its joint session in 1861, passed an act for the relief of William

H. Fannin, and whereas the said Fannin died before he could avail himself of said Act; therefore,

SECTION 1. *Be it enacted by the Senate and House of Representatives of the State of Florida in General Assembly convened,* That the representative of the said William H. Fannin, deceased, be authorized to avail himself of the provisions of said Act. Administrator, &c.

SEC. 2. *Be it further enacted,* That this Act be in force from and after its passage.

Passed the House of Representatives November 27, 1862. Passed the Senate December 4, 1862. Approved by the Governor December 6, 1862.

CHAPTER 1,334—[No. 18.]

AN ACT to change the time of holding the Spring Terms of the Circuit Courts in the counties of Walton, Holmes and Washington.

SECTION 1. *Be it enacted by the Senate and House of Representatives of the State of Florida in General Assembly convened,* That from and after the passage of this Act, the Spring Terms of the Circuit Court for Walton, Holmes and Washington, shall be held as follows: For Walton county, on the first Tuesday after the first Monday in April; for Holmes county, on the first Tuesday after the second Monday in April; for Washington county on the first Tuesday after the third Monday in April. Terms of Court.

SEC. 2. *Be it further enacted,* That all laws or parts of laws, militating against the provisions of this Act, be and the same are hereby repealed. Repeal.

Passed the House of Representatives December 1, 1862. Passed the Senate December 4, 1862. Approved by the Governor December 6, 1862.

CHAPTER 1,335—[No. 19.]

AN ACT in relation to the Courts of Escambia County and for other purposes.

SECTION 1. *Be it enacted by the Senate and House of Representatives of the State of Florida in General Assembly convened.* That from and after the passage of this act, and until the close of the war, it shall be lawful to hold the Circuit Courts, Where Court may be held.

1862.

Courts of Chancery and Probate Court of Escambia County, at Bluff Springs, in said county, at such times as in the opinion of the Judges of the respective Courts it is expedient and safe to hold said Courts.

Judge of Probate and Clerk to keep records.

SEC. 2. *Be it further enacted*, That the Judge of Probate and Clerks of the respective Courts in said county shall keep a book of record of their proceedings, which shall, after the termination of the present war, be transcribed upon the original book of records of said county and they are hereby authorized to do the same.

Removal of records.

SEC. 3. *Be it further enacted*, That the Judge of Probate, Sheriffs and Clerks are authorized to remove the records of their respective Courts to some place of safety either in or out of this State.

Other Counties included.

SEC. 4. *Be it further enacted*, That the provisions of the foregoing sections be and the same are hereby declared to be applicable to any other county in this State when it shall be deemed necessary by the Judge of the Circuit Court of the Circuit within which such county lies, and such Judge shall give due public notice of the time and place of holding Court in any other county.

Passed the Senate November 28, 1862. Passed the House of Representatives December 4, 1862. Approved by the Governor December 6, 1862.

CHAPTER 1,336—[No. 20.]

AN ACT to suspend the collection of Taxes in counties held or controlled by the Enemy.

Tax Collectors may suspend collection of taxes in certain cases.

SECTION 1. *Be it enacted by the Senate and House of Representatives of the State of Florida in General Assembly convened,* That the Tax Assessors and Collectors of those counties in this State, that are now abandoned, held, possessed or controlled by the military forces of the United States, be and they are hereby authorized and required to suspend the assessment and collection of taxes in their respective counties during and for the time that their said counties may be so possessed, held or controlled by said forces.

Counties held in part by the enemy.

SEC. 2. *Be it further enacted,* That the provisions of the first section of this Act shall be applicable to those counties the county site of which may be in possession or under the military control of the enemy, and to such sections of counties as may be in the possession or under the control of the enemy, though not entirely held by the same, in which no taxes shall be collected for the time being.

SEC. 3. *Be it further enacted*, That in all counties or parts of counties held by the forces of the United States as above declared, all taxes shall cease to accrue during and for the time that the same may be held or controlled by the enemy.

Taxes shall cease to accrue.

1862.

Passed the Senate November 28, 1862. Passed the House of Representatives Dec. 4, 1862. Approved by the Governor Dec. 6, 1862.

CHAPTER 1,337—[No. 21.]

AN ACT to aid the families of Soldiers that require Assistance.

SECTION 1. *Be it enacted by the Senate and House of Representatives of the State of Florida in General Assembly convened*, That the Governor of this State be and he is hereby authorized to cause to be issued Treasury Notes of the State of Florida from the blank notes remaining of the issue under the law approved February 14th, 1861, entitled an act providing for the issue of Treasury Notes, and of an act approved December 16th, 1861, entitled an act to provide for the payment of the War Tax to be assessed upon and collected from the citizens of this State.

Treasury notes to be issued.

SECTION 2. *Be it further enacted*, That the Governor be, and he is hereby authorized to employ a sufficient number of persons to assist in signing said notes ; and the same shall be done under the immediate supervision and control of the Governor. And records of said notes shall be kept in the same manner as is now by law provided for in the act approved December 16th, 1861, entitled an act to provide for the payment of the War Tax to be assessed upon and collected from the citizens of this State.

Persons to be employed in signing notes.

Record.

SECTION 3. *Be it further enacted*, That said Treasury notes shall be issued for the purpose of the Government, and of this issue there is hereby appropriated the sum of Two Hundred Thousand Dollars,for the relief of the disabled soldiers, and for the relief of soldiers' families that require assistance.

Purposes and appropriations for soldiers' families.

SECTION 4. *Be it further enacted*, That it shall be the duty of the several Justices of the Peace in this State to prepare lists of the families of such soldiers as are now in the military service of the Confederate States or who have been in the service of the Confederate States or of this State, or who died, were wounded or became disabled by sickness or wounds while in said service, and of all soldiers who were wounded

Judges of Probate to prepare lists, &c.

Who entitled to benefit of act.

or disabled by sickness while in either of said service, and who require assistance in their several districts, setting forth in said lists the name of the soldier and the name of each member of the family to whom the aid is to be given, and their respective ages, and said Justices of the Peace shall return said lists without delay, to the Judge of Probate, who shall consolidate the same and keep a record of the list so consolidated, and said Judge of Probate shall forward said list to the Comptroller of the State: *Provided however,* That if said Justice of the Peace or Judge of Probate, or any or either of them, shall fail or refuse so to do, or wherever there are no such officer or officers in any county of this State, the Governor shall appoint suitable persons to perform said duties, and shall cause them to be paid out of the Treasury of the county, if there be any such Treasury, if not, out of the Treasury of the State, and for which purpose the Governor shall give his order on the Comptroller, who shall issue a warrant thereon, and the Treasurer shall pay the same.

List to be forwarded to Comptroller.

Proviso.

Governor to distribute funds for benefit of soldiers' families, &c.

SECTION 5. *Be it further enacted,* That the Governor shall cause the distribution of the moneys herein appropriated to be made for the aid of the said soldiers and families, according to the necessities of the several counties in the State, being governed by his knowledge of their necessities, the prices of clothing, provisions and supplies; and the Governor shall draw his order, from time to time, upon the Comptroller for said amount; and said Comptroller shall issue his warrant for the same in favor of the County Commissioners of said county for the support of soldiers or soldiers families requiring assistance; and the Treasurer shall pay the same: *Provided however,* That wherever there is no such Board of County Commissioners in any county, or where such Board fail or refuse to perform the duties by this act enjoined, the Governor shall appoint suitable persons to perform the duties herein required of the County Commissioners, and the Comptroller shall issue his warrant, inserting their names as Trustees of the county for the purposes aforesaid.

Where there is no Board of County Commissioners.

SECTION 6. *Be it further enacted,* That the money so paid out of the Treasury shall be expended by the Board of County Commissioners or by the Trustees of the county, appointed as aforesaid, in clothing, provisions, cards, spinning wheels, and necessary family supplies for such persons as are returned on said lists, and shall cause the same to be faithfully, justly and equitably distributed, or shall pay over to

How fund to be expended.

said soldier or soldiers' family his or their *pro rata* share of said money, at their discretion.

SECTION 7. *Be it further enacted*, That in making out the list of the different families, the Judge of Probate, or person acting in his stead, shall enumerate with those who are to receive aid those who have left the county on account of invasion by the enemy, but who intend returning as soon as said invasion shall cease.

Refugees.

SECTION 8. *Be it further enacted*, That the Governor be and he is hereby authorized to appoint a suiable person for each county in the State, without delay, and shall cause to be drawn from the Treasury, by warrant of the Comptroller in favor of such person such portion of the money herein appropriated as may in his judgment, be necessary to meet the immediate wants of the soldiers and families in each county who are herein before provided for, and shall charge the same to the debit of each county. And he shall be governed in making such advance from the best evidence at his command of the number of soldiers and soldiers families aforesaid in each county, their present necessities and the inability of the county to provide for their support, and the money so advanced as aforesaid shall be deposited by the person appointed by the Governor as aforesaid and distributed as by this act is hereinbefore provided.

Governor may appoint agent.

May cause money to be advanced from the Treasury for immediate necessities.

SECTION 9. *Be it further enacted*, That the Board of County Commissioners, or Trustees of the County are hereby authorized and empowered to add to the list such person or persons as are provided for in this act, and to send amended lists from time to time to the Comptroller of the State, for the purpose of their receiving the aid intended by this act.

Additional lists.

SECTION 10. *Be it further enacted*, That the Board of County Commissioners in each county be and they are hereby requested to levy and collect the county tax heretofore authorized to be levied for the assistance of soldiers families, and to use their best endeavors to aid the State in the objects aforesaid, it not being the intention of the General Assembly to relieve the counties from any county tax which may have been levied or is authorized to be levied and collected for the support of soldiers' families.

County tax.

SECTION 11. *Be it further enacted*, That the Governor shall cause five hundred copies of this act to be printed immediately after his approval of the same, and said copies shall be distributed amongst the members of the General As-

Publication of act.

sembly for the purpose of distribution in their several counties.

Passed the Senate December 4, 1862. Passed the House of Representatives December 5, 1862. Approved December 6, 1862.

CHAPTER 1,338—[No. 22.]

AN ACT to amend the Election Laws of this State as regards the mode of voting, and for other purposes.

SECTION 1. *Be it enacted by the Senate and House of Representatives of the State of Florida in General Assembly convened,* That from and after the passage of this act, whenever a general election is held in this State, it shall be the duty of all the Inspectors at the different Precincts in each and every county, to **Ballot.** require each and every voter to have the name or names of the different candidates for whom said person may be authorized by law to vote, and the name of the office to which said voter may desire the person or persons for whom he votes to be elected, **Ballots to be numbered.** written or printed on one and the same peice of paper, which shall be numbered by the said Inspectors to correspond with the number of the name of said voter on the poll-book; and no ticket not corresponding with the foregoing requirement shall be received.

SEC. 2. *Be it further enacted,* That it shall be the duty of said **Canvass of votes.** Inspectors, as soon as the poll of an election shall have been finally closed, and before an adjournment by said Inspectors to canvass publicly the votes polled at said precincts, and after securely sealing the ballots cast at said precincts, in a separate package, and endorsing thereon ballots polled at ———— precinct on the **Returns.** —— day of ————, A. D. 18—, which shall be signed by the said Inspectors, to send in the manner now provided by law the said package, together with the usual returns, to the Judge **Canvass by Judge of Probates.** of Probate of the county, who, with the canvassers, as is now provided by law, shall, on the fifth day next, after said election was held, or sooner if the returns from all the precincts in the county shall have been received, to publicly canvass the returns that shall have been made, and make and sign certificates now required by law.

SEC. 3. *Be it further enacted,* That the said sealed packages **Packages of Ballots.** containing the ballots polled at the different precincts, shall be kept securely by the Judge of Probate of each county for twenty days from and after the day on which said election was held, when, in the presence of the Clerk and Sheriff of the Circuit Court of the county, he shall destroy the same by burning, without unsealing said packages or any of them: *Provided*, That if any candidate or candidates shall have filed a notice or notices in writing within the said twenty days with the Judge of Probate, declaring his or their intention to contest the election of any one, and protesting against the destroying the sealed packages aforesaid, it shall be the duty of the Judge of Probate to forward forthwith the said packages, together with the returns, notices and protests, enclosed in one package, endorsed "Papers relating to the contested election between —————— and ————— of ————— county, held on the —— day of —————, A. D. 18—," which shall be signed by the Judge of Probate and forwarded to the Secretary of State, who shall keep the same subject to the order of those whose duty it is by the existing laws to enquire into and decide upon contested elections: *And provided further,* That if no such notice or protest shall be filed within the twenty days aforesaid, it shall be held as conclusive as to the party or parties holding the certificates of election now required to be given by law. Contested elections.

Sec. 4. *Be it further enacted,* That paragraph number one of section number eight on page seventy-seven [77] of Thompson's Digest be so altered and amended as to read "On the thirtieth day after any general election," &c. Canvass by Secretary of State.

Sec. 5. *Be it further enacted,* That all laws or parts of laws conflicting with the provisions of this act, be and the same are hereby repealed. Repeal.

Passed the House of Representatives December 3, 1862. Passed the Senate December 5, 1862. Approved by the Governor December 8, 1862.

CHAPTER 1,339—[No. 23.]

AN ACT to prohibit Sheriffs and Clerks of the Circuit Courts of this State from appointing and having Deputies during the existence of the present war.

SECTION 1. *Be it enacted by the Senate and House of Representatives of the State of Florida in General Assembly convened,* That from and after the passage of this Act, it shall not be lawful for any Sheriff or Clerk of the Circuit Court of any county in this State to appoint, or retain in office any Deputy who is subject to the conscript law, until after a declaration of peace between this Government and that of the United States. Deputies.

SEC. 2. *Be it further enacted,* That any officer violating the first section of this Act shall, on conviction thereof before the Circuit Court of his said county, be fined in the sum of not less than five hundred dollars and not over one thousand dollars, at Penalty.

1862.

the discretion of the Court, and be removed from his said office by the Judge of the Circuit Court; *Provided*, this Act shall not go into effect until the officers herein mentioned shall have notice of the passage of this Act.

Repeal.

SEC. 3. *Be it further enacted*, That all laws and parts of laws contravening the provisions of this Act, be and the same are hereby repealed.

Passed the House of Representatives December 3, 1862. Passed the Senate December 6, 1862. Approved by the Governor December 8, 1862.

CHAPTER 1,340—[No. 24.]

AN ACT to provide for the payment of troops called into or remaining in the service of the State after the tenth day of March, 1862.

Amounts due for military service to be paid.

SECTION 1. *Be it enacted by the Senate and House of Representatives of the State of Florida in General Assembly convened*, That the Comptroller of the State be and he is hereby required to audit and allow, and the Treasurer is hereby required to pay, upon warrant from the Comptroller, all amounts found due to military companies who were called into the military service of the State subsequent to the tenth day of March, 1862, by competent authority, or who remained in said service under the direction of said authority, under the same rules and regulations as have been heretofore adopted for the payment of the military forces of the State.

Transportation, equipment and supplies.

SEC. 2. *Be it further enacted*, That the Comptroller and Treasurer shall, in like manner, audit and pay all amounts for transportation, equipments, supplies and other expenses that may have lawfully accrued against the State by or on account of the military operations of the State, subsequent to the tenth day of March, 1862, as aforesaid; *Provided*, that the whole amount of expenditure under the provisions of this Act shall not exceed the sum of twenty thousand dollars.

Passed the House of Representatives December 3, 1862. Passed the Senate December 5, 1862. Approved by the Governor December 8, 1862.

CHAPTER 1,341—[No. 25.]

AN ACT to provide for the Payment of certain Certificates issued by the State for Military services.

SECTION 1. *Be it enacted by the Senate and House of Representatives of the State of Florida in General Assembly convened*,

That the Comptroller and Treasurer shall audit, allow and pay to the holders thereof, the amount of principal and interest due on certain certificates issued under an Act to provide for the payment of Captains Sparkman's, Parker's and other volunteer companies, for service in the year 1849. Also, certificates issued under the provisions of an Act approved January 5th, 1859, entitled an Act to provide for the payment of the volunteer company of Captain Hansford D. Dyche's, and other companies therein named : *Provided*, that the amount expended under the provisions of this Act shall not exceed the amount of twenty thousand dollars, which is hereby appropriated for said purpose.

Certificates to be paid.

Proviso.

Passed the House of Representatives December 3, 1862. Passed the Senate December 5, 1862. Approved by the Governor December 8, 1862.

Chapter 1,342—[No. 26.]

AN ACT in relation to certain Certificates issued in Payment of Military services.

Section 1. *Be it enacted by the Senate and House of Representatives of the State of Florida in General Assembly convened,* That the several Tax Collectors of this State be, and they are hereby authorized and instructed to receive in payment of taxes the outstanding certificates of the Comptroller of this State, signed by T. W. Brevard, Comptroller, issued under the Act of January 5, 1859, entitled an Act to provide for the payment of the volunteer company of Captain Hansford D. Dyche's and other companies therein named, for balances due any of the citizens of this State under said Act.

Tax Collectors to receive certificates in payment of Taxes.

Passed the House of Representatives December 3, 1862. Passed the Senate December 5, 1862. Approved by the Governor December 8, 1862.

Chapter 1,343—[No. 27.]

AN ACT to Establish the Records of Calhoun County.

Section 1. *Be it enacted by the Senate and House of Representatives of the State of Florida in General Assembly convened,* That all the provisions of an Act to establish the Records of the county of Jackson and for other purposes, approved December

Records to be established.

4

1862.

Proviso.

27, 1848, except the tenth section thereof, shall be applicable to Calhoun county: *Provided*, that nothing in this Act shall prevent parties from proceeding at common law or in equity in the same manner they might have done previous to the passage of this Act.

Limitation.

Publication.

Sec. 2. *Be it further enacted*, That all proceedings to establish the records of Calhoun county under the provisions of this Act, shall be taken and commenced within four years next after the passage of this Act, and not after; *Provided, however*, that when there is no paper printed in the Circuit, notice may be given in the nearest paper.

Establishment of Record, &c., by motion.

Sec. 3. *Be it further enacted*, That it shall be lawful to establish any record lost or destroyed in said county by motion before the Court in term time, in the same manner as all other legal motions are made, heard and determined, and to sustain said motion by oral or written evidence before the Court, and the Judge thereof shall, if he be satisfied by the evidence on the motion aforesaid, order the said lost or destroyed record to be established, and said new recording shall operate *nunc pro tunc*.

Passed the House of Representatives December 3, 1862. Passed the Senate December 4, 1862. Approved by the Governor December 8, 1862.

CHAPTER 1,344—[No. 28.]

AN ACT to consolidate the offices of Clerk of the Circuit Court and Judge of Probate in and for Manatee county.

Offices consolidated.

SECTION 1. *Be it enacted by the Senate and House of Representatives of the State of Florida in General Assembly convened*, That from and after the first Monday in October, A. D. 1863, the offices of Clerk of the Circuit Court and the Judge of Probate in and for Manatee county, shall become consolidated, and the Judge of Probate shall thereafter perform all and singular the duties, and receive the fees and emoluments which appertain to the office of Clerk of the Court aforesaid.

Repeal.

Sec. 2. *Be it further enacted*, That all laws and parts of laws in conflict with this Act are hereby repealed.

Passed the House of Representatives December 3d, 1862. Passed the Senate December 5, 1862. Approved by the Governor December 8, 1862.

CHAPTER 1,345—[No. 29.]

AN ACT relative to the Assessment of Taxes.

SECTION 1. *Be it enacted by the Senate and House of Representatives of the State of Florida in General Assembly convened,* That the Board of County Commissioners of the several counties of this State shall value all property subject to taxation in their respective counties and assess the taxes thereon as required by law to be done by Tax Assessors and Collectors. {Board of County Commissioners to value property.}

SEC. 2. *Be it further enacted,* That it shall be the duty of Tax Assessors and Collectors to make a list of all the taxable property in their respective counties as provided by law, with such statistical facts concerning the same as may be requisite in estimating the value of such taxable property and make a return of the same to the Board of County Commissioners of their respective counties within the time prescribed by law for the assessment of taxes, and the County Commissioners [shall] thereupon proceed to value and assess the taxes on such property as provided in the first section of this Act : *Provided,* that nothing in this act shall be so construed as to change the present requirements of the law relative to the books of Tax Assessors and Collectors. {Tax Collectors to make lists.} {Proviso.}

SEC. 3. *Be it further enacted,* That all laws or parts of laws conflicting with the provisions of this Act be and the same are hereby repealed.

Passed the House of Representatives Nov. 27, 1862. Passed the Senate Dec. 5, 1862. Approved by the Governor Dec. 8, 1862.

CHAPTER 1,346—[No. 30.]

AN ACT to amend an Act entitled an Act to provide for the taking of Marks and Brands of Cattle driven or shipped from the counties of Sumter, Hillsboro' and Manatee.

SECTION 1. *Be it enacted by the Senate and House of Representatives of the State of Florida in General Assembly convened,* That the provisions and requirements of an Act to provide for the taking of marks and brands of cattle driven or shipped from the counties of Sumter, Hillsboro' and Manatee, approved February 13, 1861, be and the same are hereby extended and made applicable to all the counties in this State. {Act made applicable to the whole State.}

Passed the House of Representatives November 27, 1862. Passed the Senate December 5, 1862. Approved December 8, 1862.

CHAPTER 1,347—[No. 31.]

AN ACT to amend an Act entitled an Act to prevent citizens of other States from fishing in Lakes Iamonia and Miccosukie, passed 9th December, 1858.

Non-residents.

SECTION 1. *Be it enacted by the Senate and House of Representatives of the State of Florida in General Assembly convened,* That from and immediately after the passage of this Act, the words in the first section of the above recited Act, "not residents of this State," be and the same are hereby stricken out.

Repeal.

SEC. 2. *Be it further enacted,* That the entire section number two, be and the same is hereby repealed, any law to the contrary notwithstanding.

Passed the House of Representatives December 1, 1862. Passed the Senate December 6, 1862. Approved December 8, 1862.

CHAPTER 1,348—[No. 32.]

AN ACT to consolidate the offices of Sheriff, Tax Assessor and Collector in Hernando County.

Offices consolidated.

SECTION 1. *Be it enacted by the Senate and House of Representatives of the State of Florida in General Assembly convened,* That from and after the passage of this act, the Sheriff of the county of Hernando shall perform the duties of Sheriff and Tax Assessor and Collector, and that the said office of Tax Assessor and Collector as a separate and distinct office shall cease to exist, and the said Sheriff shall receive for assessing and collecting the taxes of said county, and for performing the duties required by law of the Tax Assessors and Collectors, the same compensation or commissions now allowed by law to Tax Assessors and Collectors.

Limitation.

SEC. 2. *Be it further enacted,* That this Act shall be in force from and after the time when the terms of office of the present Sheriff and Tax Collector of Hernando county shall terminate by operation of law.

Passed the House of Representatives Nov. 28, 1862. Passed the Senate Dec. 4, 1862. Approved by the Governor Dec. 8, 1862.

LAWS OF FLORIDA.

1862.

CHAPTER 1,349—[No. 33.]

AN ACT for the relief of John P. Duval.

SECTION 1. *Be it enacted by the Senate and House of Representatives of the State of Florida in General Assembly convened,* That the sum of three hundred and ninety-six dollars and sixty-six cents is hereby appropriated and set apart for the payment of John P. Duval's claim against the State for services rendered, and the Comptroller is hereby required to issue his warrant on the Treasurer in favor of the said Duval for the amount hereinbefore stated. — *Claim to be paid.*

Passed the House of Representatives November 25, 1862. Passed the Senate December 5, 1862. Approved by the Governor December 8, 1862.

CHAPTER 1,350—[No. 34.]

AN ACT to provide for the re-payment of Moneys withdrawn from the School and Seminary Funds.

SECTION 1. *Be it enacted by the Senate and House of Representatives of the State of Florida in General Assembly convened,* That the Governor of this State be, and he is hereby authorized to issue bonds of the State of Florida, in such form as he may prescribe, to be under the seal of the Treasurer and countersigned by him, payable at such time as the Governor may direct and bearing an interest of eight per cent. payable semi-annually, to the amount of the stock of the several State and other funds withdrawn by the Governor from the School and Seminary funds under the resolution authorizing the Governor to purchase arms, &c., approved on the first day of December, eighteen hundred and sixty, and not replaced in said funds, and that said bonds be deposited in the office of the Comptroller to the credit of the School and Seminary funds respectively. — *Bonds to be issued. Disposal of Bonds.*

SEC. 2. *Be it further enacted,* That the amounts which would have been due to the School and Seminary funds for the interst upon the amounts withdrawn from said funds under the resolution aforesaid, but which by reason of such withdrawal have never been paid to said funds, be passed to the credit of said funds respectively. — *Amounts due School Fund.*

SEC. 3. *Be it further enacted,* That the right is hereby reserved on behalf of the State to pay off and discharge the bonds — *Bonds may be paid.*

1862. issued in pursuance of this act before the time at which they may be made payable.

Passed the Senate Dec. 1, 1862. Passed the House of Representatives December 5, 1862. Approved by the Governor December 8, 1862.

CHAPTER 1,351—[No. 35.]

AN ACT for the Relief of James Caverly.

Payment for Hospital supplies.

SECTION. 1. *Be it enacted by the Senate and House of Representatives of the State of Florida in General Assembly convened,* That the sum of fourteen dollars and seventy-seven cents be, and the same is hereby appropriated to James Caverly, for supplies furnished to the Marine Hospital at St. Marks, for and during the year 1861, and that the Comptroller be, and he is hereby instructed to draw his warrant on the Treasurer for the same, and that it be paid out of any money in the Treasury not otherwise appropriated, any law to the contrary notwithstanding.

Passed the House of Representatives Dec. 6, 1862. Passed the Senate December 8, 1862. Approved by the Governor Dec. 10, 1862.

CHAPTER 1,352—[No. 36.]

AN ACT for the Relief of S. J. Perry, Deputy Sheriff of E. W. Vann, Sheriff of Madison county.

Claim allowed.

SECTION 1. *Be it enacted by the Senate and House of Representatives of the State of Florida in General Assembly convened,* That the Comptroller of Public Accounts be and he is hereby authorized to audit and allow the Claim of Samuel J. Perry, Deputy Sheriff of E. W. Vann, Sheriff of Madison county, amounting to the sum of one hundred dollars, being the amount due him for services in carrying Eleanor Espy, a lunatic, to the Asylum at Milledgevile, Georgia, and that he issue his warrant upon the Treasurer for the same.

Payment of account.

SEC. 2. *Be it further enacted,* That the sum of one hundred dollars, out of any monies that may be hereafter appropriated for the support and maintenance of Lunatics, be and the same is heŕeby appropriated for the payment of the account mentioned in the first section of this Act.

Passed the House of Representatives December 6th, 1862. Passed the Senate December 8th, 1862. Approved by the Governor December 10th, 1862.

CHAPTER 1,353—[No. 37.]

AN ACT for the relief of John Kelly and for other purposes.

WHEREAS, by an order of the Judge of the Circuit Court of the Middle Circuit of Florida for the county of Madison, made in the year 1859, one Susan Kelly, a lunatic, was, according to the statute, ordered to be taken by the Sheriff of Madison county to a Lunatic Asylum : *And whereas*, owing to a want of funds or a suitable appropriation for such purpose, the said Sheriff was unable to obey the order made in the premises: *And whereas*, by such default, the said Susan Kelly was remanded to the custody of her parents by said Sheriff, and has been in their care and custody up to the present time, at great expense and trouble to them : *And whereas*, the parents of said lunatic are of very limited means and are unable to bear the burthen of such a charge, which, of right, should be borne by the State according to law, therefore— *Preamble.*

SECTION 1. *Be it enacted by the Senate and House of Representatives of the State of Florida in General Assembly convened,* That the said John Kelly, the father of the said lunatic, Susan Kelly, be and he is hereby authorized to receive ten dollars per month from the first day of November, 1859, up to the present time for the care and custody of said lunatic, and ten dollars per month hereafter, annually, until such lunatic shall be sent to the Asylum or otherwise provided for by law; and that the Comptroller shall, on approving the account for the care of said lunatic, issue a warrant for the amount, to be paid out of any money in the Treasury not otherwise appropriated. *Appropriation.*

Passed the House of Representatives December 5, 1862. Passed the Senate December 8, 1862. Approved by the Governor December 10, 1862.

CHAPTER 1,354—[No. 38.]

AN ACT relating to the trial of persons in this State during the existing war.

SECTION 1. *Be it enacted by the Senate and House of Representatives of the State of Florida in General Assembly convened,*

1862.

Violations of law in counties held by the enemy.

That from and after the passage of this Act any person or persons who are guilty of the violation of any of the laws of this State, in any of the counties held or which may be held by the enemy, it shall be lawful to try said person or persons in the county nearest the one in which the offence may have been committed, in which courts may be held during the existence of the present war.

Passed the Senate December 11, 1862. Passed the House of Representatives December 13, 1862. Approved by the Governor December 13, 1862.

CHAPTER 1,355—[No. 39.]

AN ACT in relation to the County Offices of Calhoun county.

Offices, where may be kept.

SECTION 1. *Be it enacted by the Senate and House of Representatives of the State of Florida in General Assembly convened,* That the offices of the county of Calhoun, such as Sheriff, Judge of Probate, Tax-Assessor and Collector and Clerk of the Circuit Court, may be kept at the dwellings of the respective officers.

Repeal.

SEC. 2. *Be it further enacted,* That all laws and parts of laws conflicting with this be and the same are hereby repealed.

Passed the House of Representatives December 3, 1862. Passed the Senate December 8, 1862. Approved by the Governor December 10, 1862.

CHAPTER 1,356—[No. 40.]

AN ACT to authorize county offices under certain circumstances to keep their offices and records at other places than that now designated by law.

Preamble.

WHEREAS, there are now positions of our State exposed to and threatened by the incursions of an enemy, thereby endangering the safety of the public records, therefore—

County Commissioners may order removal of records.

SECTION 1. *Be it enacted by the Senate and House of Representatives of the State of Florida in General Assembly convened,* That whenever the Board of County Commissioners in any county in this State shall deem the public records unsafe at the Court House of said county, on account of the enemy, they are hereby authorized to order the several county officers to remove their respective records and to keep their offices at such place or places of safety as said Commissioners may designate, until the expiration of the present war with the United States.

Passed the House of Representatives December 6, 1862. Passed the Senate December 8, 1862. Approved by the Governor December 10, 1862.

CHAPTER 1,357—[No. 41.]

AN ACT to repeal Ordinance number fifty-two (52) of the Convention of the State of Florida entitled an ordinance for strengthening the Executive Department during the exigencies of the present war, and ordinance number fifty-eight (58) of said Convention providing the mode of filling vacancies in the Executive Council.

SECTION 1. *Be it enacted by the Senate and House of Representatives of the State of Florida in General Assembly convened,* That Ordinance number fifty-two (52) of the Convention of the State of Florida, entitled an Ordinance for strengthening the Executive Department during the exigencies of the present war, and Ordinance number fifty-eight (58) of said Convention, providing the mode of filling vacancies in the Executive Council, be and the same are hereby repealed. Repeal.

Passed the House of Representatives December 4, 1862. Passed the Senate December 5, 1862. Approved by the Governor December 10, 1862.

CHAPTER 1,358—[No. 42.]

AN ACT empowering Judges of Probate to grant orders to Executors and Administrators to sell real estate for distribution.

SECTION 1. *Be it enacted by the Senate and House of Representatives of the State of Florida in General Assembly convened,* That from and after the passage of this Act, the Judges of Probate for the several counties of this State shall have full power to Judges of Probate may order order and decree the sale of lands of all deceased persons for sale. purposes of distribution among the heirs, devisees, or legatees of such decedents.

SEC. 2. *Be it further enacted,* That when a decree or order of sale of such real estate be made by the Probate Judge, the Judge ordering the same shall require petitioner to enter into bond and Bond. sufficient security, to be approved by the court, conditioned for

5

1862.

Manner of sale.

the faithful payment and application of the money arising from said sale according to the final decree; said sales to be made by petitioner under bond and security as aforesaid, and not by commissioners as heretofore required by law.

Report and final decree.

SEC. 3. *Be it further enacted,* That when the Judge ordering sale of real estate shall receive the report of such sales, he shall determine if the conditions of sale have been complied with, and thereupon make final decree and order said petitioner or salesmen to convey the estate sold to purchaser as commissioners have been heretofore required by law to do.

SEC. 4. *Be it further enacted,* That all laws or parts of laws conflicting with the provisions of this Act, be and the same are hereby repealed.

Passed the Senate November 29, 1862. Passed the House of Representatives December 8, 1862. Approved by the Governor December 10, 1862.

CHAPTER 1,359—[No. 43.]

AN ACT to repeal an act to facilitate the construction of the St. Johns and Indian River Canal, approved January 1st, 1857, and for other purposes.

Repeal.

SECTION 1. *Be it enacted by the Senate and House of Representatives of the State of Florida in General Assembly convened,* That an Act entitled an Act to facilitate the construction of the St. Johns and Indian River Canal, approved the first day of January, 1857, be and the same is hereby repealed.

Commissioners to make Report and transfer asset to Board of Trustees Int. Improvement.

SEC. 2. *Be it further enacted,* That the Commissioners of the St. Johns and Indian River Canal be and they are hereby directed to transfer and deliver to the Board of Trustees of the Internal Improvement Fund, all goods, chattels, monies, rights, credits, books and papers, and all property of whatever kind belonging to or under the control of the said Commissioners, and release to said Trustees or otherwise convey to them, by proper and lawful deeds of conveyance, all lands and real estate now owned by said Commissioners; and the said Commissioners are directed to make to said Trustees a full report of all the doings and transactions of said Commissioners since the first day of January, 1857, and render to said Trustees a full and true account of all their receipts and expenditures since said date, and a statement of work done.

Board Int. Imp. to demand compliance with act.

SEC. 3. *Be it further enacted,* That the Trustees of the Internal Improvement Fund shall demand of the Commissioners of the St. Johns and Indian River Canal a compliance with the directions and requirements of the second section of this Act at as early a day as practicable.

1862.

SEC. 4. *Be it further enacted,* That the Trustees of the Internal Improvement Fund be and they are hereby authorized to sue for all money due to said Commissioners and to institute such proceedings in law or chancery as may be necessary to enforce or annul any contracts entered into with said Commissioners, and to carry out the provisions and requirements of this Act, and if necessary, they are hereby authorized to use the name of the State of Florida for that purpose.

Trustees of Int. Imp. Fund authorized to sue.

SEC. 5. *Be it further enacted,* That it be and it is hereby made the duty of the Board of Trustees of the Internal Improvement Fund to present to the next General Assembly, as soon as practicable after its organization, a statement of all the facts in connection with the commencement, progress and present condition of the work on said Canal, a statement of the money paid and on what account, also a statement of the lands set apart for this work by eighths of sections, and if any have been disposed of, to whom and on what terms, also a full statement of the transactions of the Canal Commissioners with regard to bonds, and a statement of the amount and actual value of work done on said Canal.

Board of Trustees to report concerning said canal.

SEC. 6. *Be it further enacted,* That all lands and property of whatever kind required to be transferred and conveyed by this Act to the Trustees of the Internal Improvement Fund, shall be held by said Trustees subject to the future action of the General Assembly.

Lands transferred.

SEC. 7. *Be it further enacted,* That the Trustees of the Internal Improvement Fund are hereby instructed to obtain from the Commissioners of the St. Johns and Indian River Canal the report of the last engineer, Mr. Burchel, relative to the practicability or impracticability of said Canal and present the same to the next General Assembly.

Report of Engineer.

SEC. 8. *Be it further enacted,* That the Attorney General shall file an application before the Supreme Court for a re-hearing in the case of the Trustees of the Internal Improvement Fund vs. William Bailey, before a competent tribunal, or by bill or otherwise, to be filed by him, shall come before a competent tribunal to have the questions in the above case settled, and the questions arising out of this Act in regard to the Indian River Canal.

Atty. General to file petition for rehearing, &c.

" Passed the House of Representatives December 5, 1862. Passed the Senate December 8, 1862. Approved by the Governor December 10, 1862.

CHAPTER 1,360—[No. 44.]

AN ACT to prevent during the existing war Monopolies, Extortions and Speculations in Bread-stuffs and other articles of general use and consumption, and to make such acts criminal, and to provide penalties for the same.

SECTION 1. *Be it enacted by the Senate and House of Representatives of the State of Florida in General Assembly convened,* That if any person shall purchase any articles of clothing, shoes, leather, cloth of any kind, provisions, wheat, flour, corn, meal, meat, bacon, hogs, cattle, salt, bagging, rope and twine sugar, syrup or molasses, or any, or either of the aforesaid articles, or any article or thing, and shall falsely represent that he, or they, is or are purchasing such article or articles for the soldiers or Government, or army of this State, or of the Confederate States, or any of the Confederate States, or shall by any fraudulent contrivance, induce, or attempt to induce the vendor to believe that he or they is, or are purchasing such article or articles for the army or Government of this State, or the Confederate States, or any of the Confederate States, such person so offending shall be guilty of a felony and upon conviction thereof in the county where the purchase may be made, shall be punished by imprisonment, not less than one year, nor longer than three years; and upon all trials for such offence, after proof of the representation shall be made, the burthen of proving the agency shall rest upon the defendant.

SEC. 2. *Be it further enacted,* That all and every person or persons who shall monopolize any of the articles above mentioned, with intent to produce a scarcity of such article or articles in the market, or of raising the price or prices of such articles, or either of them, or if any person or persons shall purchase, procure, or receive any of the articles specified in the preceding section and hold the same for the purpose of engrossing the market and raising the price of such article or articles, such person or persons so offending shall be guilty of a misdemeanor, and upon conviction thereof shall be fined in a sum not less than five hundred dollars, nor exceeding five thousand dollars.

SEC. 3. *Be it further enacted,* That if any, or either of the offences specified and described in the foregoing sections, shall be committed by a corporation through its agent, the President and Directors of such corporation, as also the agent so offering the articles for sale, shall be liable to be severally indicted for such offence, and upon conviction, shall be punished as hereinbefore prescribed.

SEC. 4. *Be it further enacted,* That any of the above articles may be purchased without the limits of this State, and imported into this State for sale, and at a price not exceeding the current

(marginal notes)
Purchasing articles under false representation.

Penalty.

Monopolies.

Engrossment.

Corporations.

Articles purchased out of the State.

prices in the neighborhood where the same shall be offered for sale.

SEC. 5. *Be it further enacted,* That it shall be the duty of the Judges of the Circuit Courts of this State, at the opening of their respective Courts, to give the provisions of this act in special charge to the Grand Jury. — *Grand Juries to be especially charged.*

SEC. 6. *Be it further enacted,* That in all indictments under this act it shall only be necessary to state the offence generally and substantially in the words of this act. — *Indictment.*

SEC. 7. *Be it further enacted,* That this act shall take effect and go into operation from and after the tenth day of its approval by the Governor, and shall continue in force for twelve months, or until the end of the present war. — *Limitation.*

Passed the Senate December 3, 1862. Passed the House of Representatives Deem er 8, 1862. Approved by the Governor December 10, 1862.

CHAPTER 1,361—[No. 45.]

AN ACT for the relief of Gen. William E. Anderson and others.

SECTION 1. *Be it enacted by the Senate and House of Representatives of the State of Florida in General Assembly convened,* That the Comptroller of the State be and he is hereby required to audit and allow, and the Treasurer is hereby required to pay upon warrant from the Comptroller, all amounts found due to General William E. Anderson and others for services rendered in the transportation of arms, ammunition, &c., from Marianna to Neil's landing in Jackson county, and also the amounts found due to Captain J. M. F. Erwin's company for services rendered in guarding, discharging and transporting of arms and ammunition on board the Steamer Florida from St. Andrews Bay to Marianna in the county aforesaid, under and by virtue of an order from his Excellency, the Governor of this State; *Provided,* that the whole amount of expenditure under the provisions of this Act shall not exceed the sum of twenty-two hundred and eighty five dollars and eight cents. — *Payment for transportation, &c. Proviso.*

Passed the House of Representatives December 5, 1862. Passed the Senate December 8, 1862. Approved by the Governor December 10, 1862.

CHAPTER 1,362—[No. 46.]

AN ACT for the relief of the widow of Gen. Benjamin Hopkins and others.

SECTION 1. *Be it enacted by the Senate and House of Representatives of the State of Florida in General Assembly convened,* That the Comptroller of this State is hereby instructed to audit and allow to the widow of General Benjamin Hopkins the pay and allowances which he would have been entitled to as Major General in the army of the United States in time of peace, if he had been in their service, for the time he was engaged in the service of the State of Florida in operations against the Indians in South Florida, in the years 1852 and 1853: *Provided,* that the pay allowed to and received by him, under the resolution approved January 8th, 1853, be deducted from the amount hereby directed to be allowed.

Payment for services in Indian war.

SEC. 2. *Be it further enacted,* That the said Comptroller audit and allow to Oscar Hart the pay and allowances of Adjutant General, allowed in the army of the United States, for the time he was engaged in the service of the State of Florida as Adjutant General in operations against the Indians in South Florida, under the command of General Hopkins, in 1852 and 1853; *Provided,* that the pay allowed to and received by him under the resolution approved January 8th, 1853, be deducted from the amount hereby directed to be allowed.

Oscar Hart.

SEC. 3. *Be it further enacted,* That the said Comptroller audit and allow to the widow of John L. Hopkins the pay and allowances of Aid-de-Camp, allowed in the army of the United States, for the time he was engaged in the service of the State of Florida as Aid-de-Camp, in operations against the Indians in South Florida, under the command of General Hopkins, in 1852 and 1853; *Provided,* that the pay allowed to and received by him under the resolution approved January 8th, 1853, be deducted from the amount hereby directed to be allowed.

Widow of J. L. Hopkins.

SEC. 4. *Be it further enacted,* That the Treasurer of this State is hereby directed to pay the warrants which shall be issued by the said Comptroller, in pursuance of the foregoing Act, out of any monies in the Treasury.

Treasurer to pay warrants.

Passed the Senate December 1, 1862. Passed the House of Representatives December 9, 1862. Approved by the Governor December 10, 1862.

CHAPTER 1,363—[No. 47.]

AN ACT to regulate Trade and Intercourse with the Indians.

SECTION 1. *Be it enacted by the Senate and House of Representatives of the State of Florida in General Assembly convened,* That the Governor of the State shall appoint an Indian Agent who shall hold his office during the pleasure of the Governor, and shall receive a salary of fifteen hundred dollars per annum, payable quarterly out of the Treasury of the State, and who shall give bond with two or more securities, to be approved by the Governor, in the penal sum of ten thousand dollars for the faithful discharge of his duties. Governor to appoint Indian Agent. Bond.

SEC. 2. *Be it further enacted,* That it shall be the duty of said agent to establish by compact or agreement with the Indians in Florida the geographical boundaries of the territory assigned to them, which are as follows, to-wit: all of the main land lying South of a line commencing at the mouth of Caloosahatchie river, thence up said river to Lake Okeechobee, thence along the Western and Northern margin of said Lake to where it is intersected by the Township line dividing Townships thirty-seven and thirty-eight, thence eastwardly along said Township line to the Atlantic Ocean. Said agent shall give to said Indians assurance of the protection of the State, and shall generally manage and superintend all intercourse with the Indians within their boundaries, agreeably to law; he shall obey all legal instructions which may be given to him by the Governor, and carry into effect such regulations as the Governor may prescribe. Boundaries of the Indian Territory. Duties of agent.

SEC. 3. *Be it further enacted,* That said agent be allowed an interpreter, to be employed by said agent at a salary of one thousand dollars per annum, to be paid out of the Treasury of this State. Interpreter.

SEC. 4. *Be it further enacted,* That it shall be the duty of said agent, as soon as he complies with the requisitions of this Act and is commissioned by the Governor, to repair with the interpreter to the Indian nation and there hold a talk with the Indians and ascertain their wishes, wants and necessities, and immediately transmit a detailed account thereof to his Excellency, the Governor, who shall then be empowered, if he shall deem it necessary, to appoint some suitable person to procure for and furnish said Indians with such articles as it may be found they stand in need of, under the direction of the Governor, and such restrictions as he may deem necessary for the full consideration of the objects contemplated by this Act; that the Governor shall have power to draw upon the Treasurer of the State at such time or times, for such amounts, as may be deemed necessary to accomplish the Duties of agent. Merchant. Articles for use of Indians. Governor may draw money.

objects of this Act, not to exceed the sum of five thousand dollars in the aggregate per annum.

Trade with Indians prohibited.

SEC. 5. *Be it further enacted,* That if any person other than such person as the Governor shall appoint shall attempt to introduce goods and trade with the Indians, he shall forfeit all merchandize offered for sale to the Indians or found in his possession, and shall moreover forfeit and pay the sum of two thousand dollars, and said merchandize may be seized by the agent.

Persons may not enter the Indian reserves.

SEC. 6. *Be it further enacted,* That no person shall pass within the Indian limits without a license therefor from the Indian Agent or remain therein longer than permitted by such license under a penalty of five hundred dollars, and the Agent shall have authority to remove from the Indian country all persons found therein contrary to law.

Stock & horses.

SEC. 7. *Be it further enacted,* That if any person shall drive or otherwise convey any stock of horses, mules, hogs or cattle to range and feed on the territory assigned to the Indians without permission of the Agent and consent of the Indians, such persons shall forfeit the sum of five dollars for each animal of such stock.

Purchases from Indians prohibited.

SEC. 8. *Be it further enacted,* That if any person other than an Indian shall, within the Indian country, purchase or receive of any Indian in the way of barter or trade, any gun or ammunition, or other article commonly used in hunting, any instrument of husbandry or cooking utensil or any article of clothing, he shall forfeit and pay the sum of five hundred dollars.

Spirituous liquors prohibited.

SEC. 9. *Be it further enacted,* That if the person appointed by the Governor to trade and barter with the Indians, or any other person shall sell, exchange, give, barter, or dispose of, any spirituous liquors or wine, to an Indian in the Indian country, or shall introduce or attempt to introduce any spirituous liquor or wine into the Indian country, such person shall forfeit and pay the sum of one thousand dollars, and it shall be lawful for any officer of the State or any Indian to take and destroy any ardent spirits or wine found in the Indian country.

Persons tampering with Indians.

SEC. 10. *Be it further enacted,* That if any person shall send, carry, or deliver any speech, message or letter to the Indians, with an intent to procure an infraction of any law of this State, or to disturb the peace and tranquility thereof, he shall forfeit and pay the sum of one thousand dollars, and be imprisoned not less than twelve months.

Crimes committed within the Indian country.

SEC. 11. *Be it further enacted,* That where, in the commission by a white person of any crime, offence or misdemeanor, within the Indian country, the property of any Indian is taken, injured or destroyed, and a conviction is had for such crime, offence or misdemeanor, the person so convicted shall be sentenced to pay to such Indian to whom the property may have belonged a sum

LAWS OF FLORIDA.

41

1862.

equal to twice the just value of the property so taken, injured or destroyed, or be imprisoned for a term not exceeding twelve months.

SEC. 12. *Be it further enacted*, That all penalties which shall accrue under this Act, shall be sued for and recovered in an action of debt, in the name of the State of Florida, before any Court having jurisdiction of the same in any county in which the defendant shall be arrested or found.

Penalties may be sued for.

SEC. 13. *Be it further enacted*, That when any goods or other property are seized by the Agent for any violation of this Act, it shall be lawful for the Agent to deliver the same to the Sheriff of the county in which they are seized, or of the nearest adjacent county where terms of the Circuit Court are held, and the Circuit Court, at the next ensuing term thereof, shall make an order for the sale of such property at such times and places, nd upon such terms as the Court shall deem best, and the seizure of the property shall be sufficient notice to the owner thereof without further service. Where the goods are of a perishable nature, the Sheriff may sell the same under the rules and regulations governing the sales of such property levied on under attachment.

Property seiz'd.

SEC. 14. *Be it further enacted*, That if any person who shall be charged with a violation of any of the provisions or regulations of this Act or with the commission of any crime, misdemeanor or offence against the laws of this State, within the Indian country, shall be found in any county of this State, such offender may be there apprehended and brought to trial, as if such crime or offence had been committed within such county: *Provided, however*, that the criminal laws of this State shall not extend to crimes committed by one Indian against another within the Indian boundary.

Persons violating this act.

Proviso.

SEC. 15. *Be it further enacted*, That the Agent shall be, and he is hereby authorized and empowered to take the depositions of witnesses touching any offences, depredations or violations of law within the purview of this Act, and to administer an oath to the deponents.

Witnesses.

SEC. 16. *Be it further enacted*, That the Governor shall be, and he is hereby authorized to prescribe rules and regulations as he may think fit for carrying into effect the provisions of this Act, and for the settlement of the accounts of the person appointed to trade and barter with the Indians.

Governor may prescribe regulations.

SEC. 17. *Be it further enacted*, That all laws and parts of laws contrary to the provisions of this Act be, and the same are hereby repealed.

Repeal.

SEC. 18. *Be it further enacted*, That this Act shall be in force from and after its passage.

Limitation.

Passed the House of Representatives December 5, 1862. Passed the Senate December 9, 1862. Approved by the Governor December 12, 1862.

6

CHAPTER 1,364—[No. 48.]

AN ACT to carry into effect the 18th Section of the 3d Article of the Constitution of the State relating to vacancies in the office of Governor.

In case of vacancy in office of Governor.

Election.

Resignation of Governor.

SECTION 1. *Be it enacted by the Senate and House of Representatives of the State of Florida in General Assembly convened,* That in case of the removal from office by death or refusal to qualify of the Governor, during the term for which he was elected, the President of the Senate or the Speaker of the House of Representatives as the case may be, who is acting as Governor according to the provisions of the Constitution, shall immediately upon assuming the duties of said office, issue his proclamation giving sixty days notice of an election to be held to fill such vacancy in said office of Governor, the canvass of said votes to be made in thirty days after said election, and the Governor elect to be qualified within fifteen days after said canvass; *Provided,* that in case the term of office to be filled by such Governor elect shall not exceed sixty days, there shall be no election ordered as above provided.

SEC. 2. *Be it further enacted,* That the resignation of the Governor shall take effect only in the way and manner herein provided. The Governor intending to resign shall issue his proclamation giving notice of his intention to resign on a day to be named therein, and ordering an election to be held to fill such intended vacancy; said election to be held in not less than sixty days from the date of said proclamation, the canvass of the votes given at said election to be counted on the thirtieth day after said election and the Governor elect to be qualified within fifteen days after said canvass, and till such Governor elect is qualified, the Governor in office shall continue to perform the duties of said office.

Passed the House of Representatives December 6, 1862. Passed the Senate December 10, 1862. Approved by the Governor December 12, 1862.

CHAPTER 1,365—[No. 49.]

AN ACT to authorize the Board of County Commissioners of the several Counties in this State to levy a specific tax for the relief of the soldiers in the service of the State or of the Confederate States.

County Commissioners authorized to levy tax.

SECTION 1. *Be it enacted by the Senate and House of Representatives of the State of Florida in General Assembly convened,* That the Board of County Commissioners of the several counties of this State be authorized and empowered to levy annually a separate and distinct tax, not exceeding one hundred per cent. on the State tax, upon all the property in their respective counties subject to taxation by the laws of this State, and appropriate the same under such rules and regulations as they may respectively prescribe, for the purchase of clothing, caps, shoes, blankets, &c., or materials out of which to manufacture the same, for the use of the soldiers from their respective counties who are or may be in the military service of the State or of the Confederate States during the existence of the present war. *Supplies for soldiers.*

SEC. 2. *Be it further enacted,* That the taxes levied under the authority conferred by the foregoing section of this Act shall be assessed and collected by the Tax Assessors and Collectors of the several counties of this State, at the same time and places, under the same rules and regulations as are prescribed by law for the assessing and collecting of the State taxes. *Assessment and collection of tax.*

SEC. 3. *Be it further enacted,* That the said several Tax Assessors and Collectors shall pay over the amount of taxes collected, under authority of this Act, to the Treasurers of their respective counties, taking their receipts for the same, and shall receive as compensation for their said services, such pay and allowance as may be annually appropriated by their respective Boards of County Commissioners. *Tax Collectors to pay over tax to County Treasurer. Compensation.*

SEC. 4. *Be it further enacted,* That the Board of County Commissioners for each county in this State be and they are hereby authorized to appropriate any balance that may be in their respective Treasuries, belonging to their county not otherwise appropriated, for the purposes enumerated in the first section of this Act, and in case there be no such balance, to borrow such amounts as they may deem necessary to meet such exigencies and necessities as may arise among their soldiery prior to making the collections hereby authorized, and pledge the faith of the county for the re-payment of the same. *Balances in county treasury.*

SEC. 5. *Be it further enacted,* That when the Captain or other commanding officer of any company from any county of this State shall notify and inform the President of the Board of County Commissioners of his county that his company or any member or members thereof are destitute of the necessary clothing, shoes, blankets, &c., and unable to procure the same from the authorities of the Confederate States, it shall be the duty of the same President, and he is hereby authorized and required forthwith to use all legitimate and proper efforts to relieve said destitution by purchasing or causing to be manufactured and forwarding by a special agent the amount of clothing, shoes, blankets, &c., necessary. *Captain notifying county Commissioners of destitution.*

SEC. 6. *Be it further enacted,* That the said several Boards of County Commissioners shall be and they are hereby required to keep a just and correct account of all monies expended by them *Account shall be kept.*

1862.

Receipts.

under authority of this Act, and upon turning over any clothing or other supplies necessary for the comfort and well being of their respective companies, the President of the respective Boards shall take or cause to be taken the receipt of the Quartermaster of the regiment to which said company may belong, specifying the number and nature of the pieces and the estimated value thereof so turned over as aforesaid, with the view of adjusting the same with the government of the Confederate States upon the establishment of peace.

Bond of Tax Collectors.

SEC. 7. *Be it further enacted,* That the official bonds of the said several Tax Assessors and Collectors shall be liable and held responsible for the faithful collection and payment of the amount of taxes assessed or received by them respectively under authority of this Act.

Passed the House of Representatives December 11, 1862. Passed the Senate December 11, 1862. Approved by the Governor December 12, 1862.

CHAPTER 1,366—[No. 50.]

AN ACT to provide for the location of Lands in lieu of cancelled Land Warrant locations.

Cancelled location of Land Warrants.

SECTION 1. *Be it enacted by the Senate and House of Representatives of the State of Florida in General Assembly convened,* That in all cases where the location of a Military Bounty Land Warrant, made prior to the act of secession, upon any of the public lands of this State was cancelled by the General Land Office at Washington, and the Land Warrant has not been returned to the person locating the same, and where such locations may hereafter be cancelled, the person owning said Land Warrant shall have the right to locate other lands to the amount granted in said warrant, in the same manner and under the same regulations as though said Warrant was in his possession; *Pro-*

Proviso.

vided, however, That this act shall not apply to locations cancelled for any defect in the Warrant itself, or the assignment thereof.

Passed the House of Representatives December 8, 1862. Passed the Senate December 10, 1862. Approved by the Governor December 12, 1862.

CHAPTER 1,367—[No. 51.]

AN ACT to prevent the entry of Lands occupied by Soldiers or their Families during the continuance of the present war, and also to regulate the entry and sale of Public Lands.

SECTION 1. *Be it enacted by the Senate and House of Representatives of the State of Florida in General Assembly convened,* That the Register of Public Lands be and he is hereby required to suspend all further entries of lands which are occupied by soldiers in the service of this State or of the Confederate States, or by their families, during the continuance of the present war; and that any entries of lands so made, subsequent to the passage of this act, by accident, mistake, or want of information on the part of either the Register or Receivers, be and the same are hereby declared voidable upon application to the Register by the soldier or his family, who resides on such lands so entered, or their duly authorized agent; *Provided,* That the provisions of this act shall be limited to one hundred and sixty acres of land so occupied or settled by a soldier or his family; *And provided further,* That the claimant shall have three years from the close of the war in which to pay for the land.

(marginal note: Sale of lands occupied by soldiers, suspended.)

(marginal note: Proviso.)

SEC. 2. *Be it further enacted,* That the lands derived from the United States by secession, shall be restored to market on the first Monday in April, eighteen hundred and sixty-three, and subject to entry at one dollar per acre, except hammock lands, which shall be subject to entry at two dollars per acre.

(marginal note: Sale of lands.)

(marginal note: Price.)

SEC. 3. *Be it further enacted,* That the Register be and he is hereby required to give thirty days notice in each county in the State where these lands are situated, by advertising in a newspaper published in or nearest the county, and by putting a notice in at least three public places, one of which, if it is practicable, shall be near the front of the Court House.

(marginal note: Notice of sale.)

SEC. 4. *Be it further enacted,* That when such lands are restored to market, any person who may have cultivated and improved any part thereof, shall be entitled to enter the same in preference to other applicants; *Provided,* That such preference shall only extend to one hundred and sixty acres; *Provided, also,* That the settler shall make application within twelve months from the time such lands shall be subject to entry.

(marginal note: Cultivated and improved lands.)

(marginal note: Proviso.)

SEC. 5. *Be it further enacted,* That all citizens of this State holding land warrants derived from or under any act of the United States, prior to the secession of this State, who shall have been in possession of said warrant prior to said act of secession, or warrants issued to citizens of this State after secession, shall have the right to locate such warrant upon any lands subject to entry under the provisions of this act.

(marginal note: Citizens holding land Warrants.)

Lands entered
after Jan'y 10.
1861.

Proviso.

Location of
Salesman and
Receiver's offi-
cers.

Entries of lands
by soldiers.

Proviso.

Lands entered
by soldiers.

Repeal.

SEC. 6. *Be it further enacted,* That all persons who entered lands or located land warrants at the late United States Land Office in this State, after the tenth day of January, eighteen hundred and sixty-one, shall be allowed to enter said lands from the State and pay for the same, at the price originally paid, and to locate said warrants upon the same lands upon which they were originally located; *Provided,* That such entries and locations would have been legal under the laws and regulations of the United States had the State not seceded.

SEC. 7. *Be it further enacted,* That the Salesman or Receiver's Offices for the several Circuits in this State, shall be located as follows: That of the Western Circuit at Euchecanna; that of the Suwannee Circuit at Newnansville; that of the Eastern Circuit at Orange Springs, during the war, and after the war at Palatka; and that of the Southern Circuit at Tampa, or at any other point in Hillsborough where the Receiver may consider it of greater safety; and it shall be the duty of the said Salesman or Receivers to keep their offices at said places respectively.

SEC. 8. *Be it further enacted,* That all persons who shall have served as soldiers during the present war, shall have the right to enter any of the lands derived by the act of secession, not exceeding one hundred and sixty acres, at the rate of fifty cents per acre, for any lands lying within six miles of a navigable river or route of a Railroad as aforesaid, and twenty cents per acre for any lands lying beyond six miles from such river or railroad route; *Provided,* That said entry shall not be made until two years of actual residence upon said land, and proofs of said residence shall have been rendered to the satisfaction of the Register of Public Lands.

SEC. 9. *Be it further enacted,* That lands entered by the soldiers as aforesaid, shall not be subject to sale under execution during the life-time of the holder; *Provided,* He continues to occupy said land.

SEC. 10. *Be it further enacted,* That all laws and parts of laws inconsistent with this act, be and the same are hereby repealed.

Passed the Senate Dec. 8, 1862. Passed the House of Representatives December 11, 1862. Approved by the Governor December 13, 1862.

CHAPTER 1,368—[No. 52.]

AN ACT in relation to the issue of patents to lands entered in this State prior to the date of secession of the State of Florida.

SECTION 1. *Be it enacted by the Senate and House of Representatives of the State of Florida in General Assembly con-*

LAWS OF FLORIDA.

vened, That from and after the passage of this Act, all persons having certificates of entry for lands entered by them or any other person, and they owning the same, and there cannot be any patent found in any of the land offices, it shall be the duty of the Register of Public Lands to issue a patent in the name of said person presenting the same, provided the entries on the books correspond with said certificates.

Register to issue patent.

SEC. 2. *Be it further enacted,* That the person so applying for said grant or patent shall pay the Register the sum of fifty cents for so issuing said patent or patents; said patents to be signed by the Governor and countersigned by the Register of Public Lands.

Register to receive fee for issuing patent.

SEC. 3. *Be it further enacted,* That all laws or parts of laws conflicting against this Act be and the same are hereby repealed.

Repeal.

Passed the House of Representatives December 6, 1862. Passed the Senate December 10, 1862. Approved by the Governor December 13, 1862.

CHAPTER 1,369—[No. 53.]

AN ACT to re-establish the records of any county in this State which have been lost, mislaid or destroyed.

SECTION. 1. *Be it enacted by the Senate and House of Representatives of the State of Florida in General Assembly convened,* That it shall be lawful, when any person whose titles, deeds, bonds, mortgages, conveyances, receipts, or other papers required or authorized by law to be recorded, and which have been of record or on file for record in any county in this State and lost, mislaid or destroyed, who shall produce a paper writing purporting to be a copy, or as near as may be known or recollected, a copy of the original paper so lost, mislaid or destroyed as aforesaid, with full or circumstantial proof of the substance thereof, and of his or her title thereto, or interest therein, and shall file the same in the office of the Clerk of the Circuit Court or recording officer of the county where such paper was recorded or filed for record, and serve on the opposite party to be affected thereby a copy thereof, or give notice by advertisement in a newspaper published in the Circuit of which said county is a part, or if no newspaper is published in said Circuit, in a newspaper publihsed in the nearest Circuit, for the space of three months, that such person intends to establish such title, deed, bond, mortgage, conveyance, receipt or other paper required or authorized by law to be recorded, in case no sufficient objection be made, for the Circuit Court of said county at its first term af-

Records lost or destroyed.

Copy.

Notice.

Establishment of record.

Proviso.

ter giving such notice to establish the title and right of such person and admit again to record such papers so established as aforesaid: *Provided,* That nothing contained in this section shall be so construed as to prohibit the recoording of any paper authorized or required by law to be recorded, upon the presentation of the original with the Clerk's certificate of record thereon.

Marks and brands.

SEC. 2. *Be it further enacted,* That to re-establish the record of marks and brands, lost, mislaid or destroyed as aforesaid, the person making such application shall make, before the Clerk of the Circuit Court or recording officer of said county, an affidavit stating the particular mark and brand recorded and so lost, mislaid or destroyed, and as near as may be known or recollected, the time when the same was recorded.

Record of Marriages.

SEC. 3. *Be it further enacted,* That to re-establish the record of marriages lost, mislaid or destroyed, the person making such application shall make an affidavit before the Clerk of the Circuit Court of said county, stating the names of the persons married, the name and officer who administered the marriage ceremony, the officer from which the license was issued, and as near as may be the date of the license, which affidavit shall be filed and recorded in the Clerk's office of said county.

Wills and letters testamentary, &c.

SEC. 4. *Be it further enacted,* That to re-establish record of any will, letters testamentary of administration or guardianship, of assignment of dower, or any other paper or papers, or any instrument of writing or judgment, order or decree of the Probate Court or Judge in any way connected with the administration of the estate of any decedent, or the administration of guardians authorized or required by law to be recorded, and which have been of record, or on file for record, in any Probate office in this State and which have been lost, mislaid or destroyed, the applicant shall produce the original or a paper writing purporting to be a copy, or as near as may be known or recollected, a copy of the original paper or record so lost, mislaid or destroyed, with full or circumstantial proof of the substance thereof, accompanied with a declaration of his intention to establish such record or paper so lost, mislaid or destroyed, and shall notify the opposite party or persons interested, in the manner provided in the first section of this Act, and at the first term of the Circuit Court thereafter, if no sufficient objection be made, such record or paper so lost, mislaid or destroyed, shall, by order of said Court, be re-established and again admitted to record.

Judgments and decrees.

SEC. 5. *Be it further enacted,* That in all cases where judgments at law or decrees in chancery have been entered or recorded in the County, Superior or Circuit Courts of any county in this State, the evidence of which shall have been lost, mislaid or destroyed, it shall and may be lawful for the plaintiff or party interested therein by himself or his attorney, to file his certain petition upon oath stating the facts in such case, which petition shall be filed three months previous to any term of the Circuit Court of said county, and a copy thereof shall be served in the same manner as other legal process, at least sixty days before any term as aforesaid at which any action upon the same shall take place upon the defendant or his representatives.

SEC. 6. *Be it further enacted*, That whenever it shall be made to appear by affidavit to the Judge of the Circuit Court that any party defendant or his representatives reside beyond the limits of this State, it shall be lawful for said Judge to order a hearing on the facts charged in said petition, and thereupon to pass an order in the same manner as though said defendant had appeared and were present in Court: *Provided*, That a copy of said order for the hearing shall have been first served upon the said defendant, his authorized agent, or legal representative, sixty days before the time fixed for the said hearing, or be published in some newspaper in said Circuit, or if there be no newspaper in said Circuit, in a newspaper published in some other Circuit, for the term of three months, or such longer time as the Judge may direct.

Non-res i d e n t parties defendant.

SEC. 7. *Be it further enacted*, That defendant's answer shall be filed within sixty days from the date of the service of a copy of said petition, or in case of publication of an order for hearing, shall be filed at least thirty days before the day fixed for the hearing of the same.

Answer of defendant.

SEC. 8. *Be it further enacted*, That it shall be the duty of the Judge of said county, upon being satisfied that notice has been given as aforesaid, to hear the same upon the petition and answers, or petition and evidence adduced if there be no answer, and summary proceedings shall thereupon be had to establish such judgment or decree in such manner as the Court may direct, and the judgment or decree which may thereupon be rendered by the said Court, if in favor of the petitioner, shall be deemed as re-establishing such judgment or decree to all intents and purposes as the same existed at the time of the loss or destruction of the evidence of the same, and if upon the hearing of said petition it shall appear to the satisfaction of the Court, by the affidavit of the petitioner or otherwise, that an execution had issued upon said judgment or decree, and that said execution had been lost, mislaid or destroyed, and not paid or satisfied, the said Court shall incorporate in its judgment re-establishing such judgment or decree an order that another execution be issued.

Hearing o cause.

Judgment a n d orders.

SEC. 9. *Be it further enacted*, That when the documents, papers and instruments of writing pertaining to proceedings and matters pending and undetermined in any Court in this State, shall be lost, mislaid or destroyed, all such papers, documents

Re-establishment of lost papers.

7

1862.

and instruments of writing may be re-established in the manner prescribed by law in reference to lost papers, or in the manner pointed out in this Act, or in such manner as the Court shall specially direct.

Seal destroyed.

Sec. 10. *Be fit urther enacted*, That whenever the seal of office of the Clerk of the Circuit Court or Judge of Probate of any county in this State shall have been or may hereafter be destroyed, his private seal shall be sufficient in all cases where a seal is required by law, until a seal of office is provided for said Court.

Deeds.

Sec. 11. *Be it further enacted*, That all proceedings taken under the provisions of the first section of this Act, so far as deeds and other conveyances of real estate are concerned, shall be taken and commenced within four years next after the said deeds or other conveyances shall have been lost, mislaid or destroyed, and not after.

Proceedings in Equity.

Sec. 12. *Be it further enacted*, That nothing in this Act contained shall prevent the persons from proceeding at common law or in equity for the re-establishment of records or papers in the same manner they might have done previous to the passage of this Act.

Repeal.

Sec. 13. *Be it further enacted*, That all laws and parts of laws contravening the provisions of this act, be and the same are hereby repealed.

Passed the House of Representatives December 8, 1862. Passed the Senate December 11, 1862. Approved by the Governor December 13, 1862.

CHAPTER 1,370—[No. 54.]

AN ACT to protect the interest of Stock owners in this State.

Section 1. *Be it enacted by the Senate and House of Representatives of the State of Florida in General Assembly convened,* That from and after the passage of this Act, the owners of such slaves as shall be convicted of stealing or killing any animal or animals whatever, belonging to any white person in this State, shall be compelled to pay the owner or owners thereof the full value of the same, to be assessed by the Court.

Own'rs of slaves made responsible, &c.

Passed the Senate December 9, 1862. Passed the House of Representatives December 12, 1862. Approved by the Governor December 13, 1862.

CHAPTER 1,371—[No. 55.]

AN ACT appropriating the sum of twenty-five thousand dollars for the sick and wounded soldiers from Florida in the several Hospitals.

SECTION 1. *Be it enacted by the Senate and House of Representatives of the State of Florida in General Assembly convened,* That the sum of twenty-five thousand dollars be and it is hereby appropriated for the benefit of the sick and wounded soldiers from Florida in the several hospitals in this State and the Confederate States, and the same shall be paid on warrant of the Comptroller by the Treasurer, and the Comptroller shall issue his warrant on the order of the Governor, and the Governor shall cause this appropriation to be distributed to the several hospitals aforesaid, as equally as the nature of the case will permit.

Appropriation.

Governor to distribute appropriation.

Passed the Senate December 8, 1862. Passed the House of Representatives December 10, 1862. Approved by the Governor December 13, 1862.

CHAPTER 1,372—[No. 56.]

AN ACT to provide for an additional issue of Treasury Notes.

SECTION 1. *Be it enacted by the Senate and House of Representatives of the State of Florida in General Assembly convened,* That the Governor be and he is hereby authorized and required to issue, in accordance with the provisions of an act entitled "an act providing for the issue of Treasury Notes, approved February 14th, 1861," the additional sum of three hundred thousand dollars, fifty thousand of which shall be issued in fractional parts of a dollar, and the balance in denominations of ones, twos, threes, fives, tens, twenties, fifties and hundreds, in the following proportions, to-wit: thirty thousand in ones, thirty thousand in twos, thirty thousand in threes, thirty thousand in fives, thirty thousand in tens, twenty-five thousand in twenties, twenty-five thousand in fifties, and fifty thousand in hundreds, for the purpose of defraying the necessary expenses of Government.

Treasury notes to be received.

Denominations.

SEC. 2. *Be it further enacted,* That from and after the passage of this act, it shall be unlawful for any individual or corporation in this State, unless expressly authorized by law so to do, to issue or put in circulation notes or change bills of the denomination of one dollar or any fractional part of a dollar, or any certificate of deposit or other paper intended to pass as money or currency, which are now unauthorized by law; and any person or corpora-

Notes and change bills, certificates of deposit, &c.

1862.

Penalty.

tion offending against the provisions of this act, shall be liable to indictment for the same, and on conviction, shall be fined in a sum not exceeding five thousand dollars, at the discretion of the jury; and any banking or other corporation offending against the same, shall be subject to a forfeiture of its charter.

Circulation of change bills, &c., prohibited.

Penalty.

SEC. 3. *Be it further enacted,* That from and after ninety days after the approval of this act, it shall not be lawful for any person to circulate or pay out any change bill or bills, note or notes, certificate or certificates of desposit, the issue of which is prohibited by the second section of this act; and any person violating this provision of law, shall be guilty of a misdemeanor, and upon conviction, shall be fined in a sum not exceeding one thousand dollars, at the discretion of the jury.

Passed the House of Representatives December 9, 1862. Passed the Senate December 11, 1862. Approved by the Governor December 13, 1862.

CHAPTER 1,373—[No. 57.]

AN ACT for the relief of Capt. Jenkins, of the Sloop Hancock.

Comptroller to issue Warrant, &c.

SECTION 1. *Be it enacted by the Senate and House of Representatives of the State of Florida in General Assembly convened,* That the Comptroller of this State be and he is hereby authorized and required to issue his warrant on the Treasury for the sum of two hundred and forty dollars in favor of C. T. Jenkins, of the sloop Hancock, for services rendered the State in the year 1861, on his producing the necessary certificates therefor, and that the Treasurer pay the same.

Passed the House of Representatives December 10, 1862. Passed the Senate December 10, 1862. Approved by the Governor December 12, 1862.

CHAPTER 1,374—[No. 58.]

AN ACT for the relief of Dr. James S. Meredith.

Claim to be allowed.

SECTION 1. *Be it enacted by the Senate and House of Representatives of the State of Florida in General Assembly convened,* That the Comptroller be authorized to audit, on presentation of the proper vouchers or certificates of his claim, and the Treasurer to pay to Dr. James S. Meredith the amount due him for serving as Assistant Surgeon in State service, provided it does not exceed eighty dollars.

Passed the House of Representatives December 10, 1862. Passed the Senate December 12, 1862. Approved by the Governor December 13, 1862.

CHAPTER 1,375—[No. 59.]

AN ACT for the relief of Lieutenant Henry A. Gray.

SECTION 1. *Be it enacted by the Senate and House of Representatives of the State of Florida in General Assembly convened,* That the Comptroller be authorized to audit and the Treasurer to pay to Lieutenant Henry A. Gray the amount due him for the use of the Steamer Emma while impressed into the service of the State, by order of John Westcott, Aid to General Pyles, provided the same does not amount to more than one hundred and twenty dollars.

Claim to be paid.

Passed the House of Representatives December 10, 1862. Passed the Senate December 11, 1862. Approved by the Governor December 13, 1862.

CHAPTER 1,376—[No. 60.]

AN ACT for the relief of John A. Granger.

SECTION 1. *Be it enacted by the Senate and House of Representatives of the State of Florida in General Assembly convened,* That the Comptroller be authorized to audit and the Treasurer to pay the amount due John A. Granger for serving in Captain B. Hopkins Company of Cavalry, in State service, from 19th October to 15th November, 1861, inclusive, provided it does not exceed twenty four dollars and thirty seven cents.

Claim to be paid.

Passed the House of Representatives December 11, 1862. Passed the Senate December 12, 1862. Approved by the Governor December 13, 1862.

CHAPTER 1,377—[No. 61.]

AN ACT to provide for a Hospital for Florida Troops in the army of the West.

SECTION 1. *Be it enacted by the Senate and House of Representatives of the State of Florida in General Assembly convened,*

1862.

Appropriation.

That the sum of ten thousand dollars be and the same is hereby appropriated, out of any monies in the Treasury not otherwise appropriated, for the purpose of providing a Hospital at Atlanta, Chattanooga, or some other convenient and suitable place, for the benefit of Florida troops in the West.

Governor to em ploy agents.

Proviso.

SEC. 2. *Be it further enacted*, That the Governor be and he is hereby authorized and empowered to employ the necessary number of agents to make all needful arrangements to carry into effect the intent and purposes of this Act: *Provided*, that the amount above appropriated shall be drawn from the Treasury by the Governor, under a warrant from the Comptroller, in such sums as in his judgment the necessities of the case may require.

Passed the House of Representatives December 13, 1862. Passed the Senate December 13, 1862. Approved by the Governor December 15, 1862.

CHAPTER 1,378—[No. 62.]

AN ACT to facilitate the Construction of Public Defence.

Owner of slave property to furnish labor on requisition of Governor.

SECTION 1. *Be it enacted by the Senate and House of Representatives of the State of Florida in General Assembly convened*, That if the Confederate authorities shall call upon the Governor of this State for laborers to construct or aid in the construction and completion of any works by them deemed necessary for the public defence, it shall be lawful for and is hereby made the duty of the Governor to issue his order requiring all owners of slave property to send to the point indicated by him the amount of slave laborers required of him or them.

Duty of slave owners.

SEC. 2. *Be it further enacted*, That upon the issuing and publication of said order, it shall be the duty of all owners of slaves as aforesaid, to send to the point indicated the amount of labor called for in said order.

Labor may be impressed.

SEC. 3. *Be it further enacted*, That in case of the failure or refusal of any owner or owners to furnish the laborers called for, it, shall be the duty of the Governor to impress such labor and send the same to the point indicated.

Arrangement between the State and Confederate authorities.

SEC. 4. *Be it further enacted*, That the Governor shall not issue the order required by this act until satisfactory arrangements shall have been entered into between the Confederate authorities and himself for just and reasonable compensation for the services of the laborers so employed, for their being well and sufficiently supplied with rations, properly sheltered, duly provided for in case of sickness, and such other details as the Governor may deem necessary to preserve the rights and property of said owners.

SEC. 5. *Be it further enacted,* That the Governor is hereby authorized to make all rules and regulations necessary to the faithful carrying out the provisions of this Act. Rules and regulations.

SEC. 6. *Be it further enacted,* That it shall be the duty of the person delivering any slave or slaves to the Confederate officer, under the provisions of this bill, to take his receipt therefor, stating the name, age and probable value thereof. Receipt.

SEC. 7. *Be it further enacted,* That all necessary expenses incurred in sending slaves to the point or points indicated by the officer calling therefor, shall be a proper charge against the Confederate government. Expenses.

Passed the House of Representatives December 6, 1862. Passed the Senate December 11, 1862. Approved by the Governor December 15, 1862.

CHAPTER 1,379—[No. 63.]

AN ACT to authorize the canvass of returns of elections held by the troops in the service of this State or of the Confederate States.

SECTION 1. *Be it enacted by the Senate and House of Representatives of the State of Florida in General Assembly convened,* That in all elections for Representatives in the General Assembly of this State held in military camps, under the provisions of Ordinance No. 53, of the Convention of said State, the officer highest in command, being a citizen of Florida, shall designate as many places for voting within the post or encampment as there are counties in the State from which the men came, who compose said command; and no person of one county shall vote at any place designated for those of another county to vote, under the pains and penalties imposed by the laws of this State for fraudulent voting. Officer to designate places for voting.

SEC. 2. *Be it further enacted.* That the provisions of an act entitled "an act to amend the elections laws of this State as regards the mode of voting, and for other purposes," approved on the 8th day of December, 1862, shall be, and the same are, so far as they can be applicable, hereby extended to all elections held in military camps under the ordinance aforesaid. Act of 1862.

SEC. 3. *Be it further enacted,* That returns of all elections held in said military camps under said ordinance shall, immediately after the closing of the polls and the canvass and count of the votes, be certified and sealed up, with the ballots given in said election, and shall be endorsed "Election Returns," as provided Returns.

for by law, and directed to the Judge of Probate of the county
from which the men came, who may have voted in said election,
if said election was for Representatives in the General Assembly,
but if said election was for Representative in Congress and for
Senators of the General Assembly of this State, then said election returns shall be directed to the Secretary of State; and in
every case said election returns shall be sent by a trusty person,
to be appointed by the officer in command aforesaid, which person shall be sworn by the Inspectors faithfully to deliver said
"Election Returns" to the Post Master at the nearest Post Office,
to be transmitted by mail to the Judge of Probate or Secretary
of State, as the case may be; and all postage which shall be paid
by such person on any package containing said "Elections Returns," shall be audited and allowed by the Comptroller of this
State on presentation of the receipt of the Post Master for such
package with his post office stamp affixed; and in case such person shall fail to deliver said "Elections Returns" to the Post
Master, as above provided for, he shall suffer the pains and penalties provided and imposed by the laws of this State for failing
or refusing to deliver "Election Returns" when sent from Precincts in this State to the Court House or seat of justice.

Canvass of votes. SEC. 4. *Be it further enacted*, That the Board of County Canvassers provided for by law shall, on the twentieth day after any
election for Representatives in the General Assembly, proceed
to canvass and count the votes given in said military camps; and
the Judge of Probate shall, upon the close thereof, make and
deliver the certificate provided for by law to the person chosen
Certificate. at said election, and shall also make and transmit the returns and
other papers to the Secretary of State in conformity to law.

Burning of Packages of ballots. SEC. 5. *Be it further enacted*, That during the continuance of
the war, Judges of Probate shall suspend the burning of the
packages of ballots as provided for by law until the expiration of
thirty days after the election.

Representative. SEC. 6. *Be it further enacted*, That to avoid all confusion hereafter, the word "Assemblymen," wherever it occurs in the laws
of this State, be annulled, and the words "Representative in the
General Assembly" and "Representative," as the case may require, be substituted therefor.

Repeal. SEC. 7. *Be it further enacted*, That all laws and parts of laws,
and all parts of said Ordinance No. 53, conflicting with the provisions of this act, be and the same are hereby repealed.

Passed the Senate December 15, 1862. Passed the House of Representatives
December 15, 1862. Approved by the Governor December 15, 1862.

LAWS OF FLORIDA.

CHAPTER 1,380—[No. 64.]

AN ACT to amend "an act to authorize the Board of County Commissioners of the several counties in this State to levy a specific tax for the relief of the soldiers in the service of the State or of the Confederate States," approved December 12, 1862.

SECTION 1. *Be it enacted by the Senate and House of Representatives of the State of Florida in General Assembly convened,* That the 5th section of an Act entitled an Act to authorize the Board of County Commissioners of the several counties in this State to levy a specific tax for the relief of the soldiers in the service of the State or of the Confederate States, approved December 12, 1862, be and the same is hereby repealed, and that the following shall be in lieu thereof, viz: That when the Captain or other commanding officer of any company from any county of this State shall notify and inform the President of the Board of County Commissioners of his county that his company, or a majority of the members thereof, are destitute of the necessary clothing, shoes, blankets, &c., and unable to procure the same from the authorities of the Confederate States, it shall be the duty of the said President and Board of County Commissioners, and they are hereby authorized and required forthwith to use all legitimate and proper efforts to relieve said destitution by purchasing or causing to be manufactured and forwarding promptly, with the least possible expense, the amount of clothing, shoes, blankets, &c., necessary to relieve the destitution complained of, and said Board of County Commissioners shall cause all the expenses and the cost thereof to be defrayed and paid out of the Treasury of their county.

5th section repealed.

County Commissioners to relieve destitute soldiers.

Passed the House of Representatives December 13, 1862. Passed the Senate December 15, 1862. Approved December 15, 1862.

CHAPTER 1,381—[No. 65.]

AN ACT to facilitate the collection of debts due the State by any officers.

SECTION 1. *Be it enacted by the Senate and House of Representatives of the State of Florida in General Assembly convened,* That whenever any officer, civil or military, is indebted to the State, the same shall be recovered against such officer and his securities upon motion before the Circuit Court, to be made by the Solicitor or Attorney appointed by the Governor. At the

Mode of recovery of amounts due the State.

8

first term a rule *nisi* shall be granted by the Judge upon the motion aforesaid, and said rule *nisi* shall issue against the officer and his securities, and at the second term the Court shall try and hear said cause upon the answer to said rule, and in default of an answer being filed, the Court shall cause Judgment to be entered against said officer and his securities for the amount due by said officer to the State of Florida; and whenever an answer is filed, the Court, after the cause is determined, shall cause judgment to be entered against the officer and his securities; *Provided, however*, that a Jury shall be empanelled to try the facts as in other cases.

Passed the Senate December 15, 1862. Passed the House of Representatives Dec. 15, 1862. Approved by the Governor Dec. 15, 1862.

CHAPTER 1,382—[No. 66.]

AN ACT to prevent the establishment of distilleries and the distilling of Whiskey or other spirituous liquors.

SECTION 1. *Be it enacted by the Senate and House of Representatives of the State of Florida in General Assembly convened,* That from and after the passage of this act, it shall be unlawful for any person or persons to erect, put up or establish, within this State, any Distillery for the purpose of distilling therein any alcohol, whiskey or other spirituous liquors, or for any person or persons to distil any alcohol, whiskey or other spirituous liquors in any still owned, leased, hired, or used by him or them, within the State; and any person offending against any of the provisions of this section, shall be liable to indictment, and on conviction before a Court of competent jurisdiction, be fined in a sum not less than one thousand dollars or more than five thousand dollars, or imprisoned not less than three months or more than twelve months, at the discretion of the Court.

SEC. 2. *Be it further enacted,* That it shall be the duty of the Governor, and he is hereby authorized and required to proceed forthwith and in the most summary manner, to abate as a nuisance any distillery at work in this State contrary to the provisions of this act, and to cause the arrest and examination of any person or persons distilling as aforesaid, and to seize all liquor distilled contrary to the provisions of this act and turn over the same to hospital uses.

SEC. 3. *Be it further enacted,* That nothing in this act contained shall prevent the distilling of alcohol, whiskey or other spirituous liquor for the actual use of the army of the Confeder-

Marginal notes:
Distilleries and distillation prohibited.

Penalty.

Governor to suppress distilleries, &c.

Spirituous liquors for use of the army and government.

ate States; *Provided*, That the person or persons desiring to distil for the use of the Confederate States shall, before erecting a still or proceeding to distil as aforesaid, exhibit to the Governor of the State the contract entered into between him or them and the proper department of the Confederate States, and upon the exhibition of such contract, and said party or parties giving good and sufficient bond in the penal sum of twenty thousand dollars conditioned not to distil for any private person or persons or for any orup on any contract or obligation other than the one exhibited to the Governor as aforesaid, and not to dispose of any alcohol, whiskey or other spirituous liquor to any person or persons except for medicinal purposes, application being made upon a certificate of a practicing physician or the President of the Board of County Commissioners, the Governor may issue his license to him or them upon the terms and conditions aforesaid; *And provided further*, That immediately upon information being communicated to the Governor of the infraction of any part of said license, he shall proceed at once to abate such distillery in the manner provided in the second section of this act, and also to cause the bond to be properly and efficiently prosecuted.

Medicinal purposes.

Passed the Senate December 12, 1862. Passed the House of Representatives December 13, 1862. Approved by the Governor December 15, 1862.

CHAPTER 1,383—[No. 67.]

AN ACT making appropriations for the expenses of the First Session of the Twelfth General Assembly, and for other purposes.

SECTION 1. *Be it enacted by the Senate and House of Representatives of the State of Florida in General Assembly convened,* That the following sums shall be paid out of any monies in the Treasury not otherwise appropriated to the following named persons, to-wit: To E. J. Vann, President of the Senate, $243 20; James Abercrombie, Senator 1st District, $150 00; A. K. Allison, Senator, $149 40; J, M. Arnow, Senator, $187 00; J. P. Carter, Senator, $148 20; J. D. Clary, Senator, $185 00; J. G. Cooper, Senator, $185 00; D. P. Hogue, Senator, $145 00; D. P. Holland, Senator, $185 00; Edward Hopkins, Senator, $178 00; J. L. King, Senator, $172 00; Jesse Norwood, Senator, $160 00; W. C. Roper, Senator, $200 00; J. S. Russell, Senator, $151 00; T. T. Russell, Senator, $192 60; J. Scott, Senator, $195 00; J. B. Smith, Senator, $161 00; J. M. Taylor, Senator, $209 00; E. J. Judah, Secretary of the Senate, $187 50; T. S. Haughton, Assistant Secretary of the Senate, $188 50; J. L. Tatum, En-

Appropriation.

Senate.

1862.

grossing Clerk, $145 00; E. M. West, Enrolling Clerk, $145 00; J. Brass, Recording Clerk, $153 90; J. White, Sergeant-at-Arms and Doorkeeper, $206 90; R. E. Frier, Messenger, $155 70; To T. J. Eppes, Speaker of the House, $273 00; A. Richardson, Representative, $245 00; S. R. Sessions, Representative, $164 00;

House of Representatives. John F. Jackson, Representative, $195 00; W. B. Ross, Representative, $166 00; W. C. Newbern, Representative, $170 00; J. A. Lee, Representative, $205 00; G. W. Blackburn, Representative, $152 60; J. C. Greeley, Representative, $190 40; R. T. H. Thomas, Representative, $195 00; T. J. McGehee, Representative, $163 00; A. Y. Hampton, Representative, $157 00; Neil Hendry, Representative, $163 00; T. Baltzell, Representative, $145 00; John G. Smith, Representative, $185 00; F. R. Pittman, Representative, $159 00; W. Chapman, Representative, $159 00; Felix Leslie, Representative, $160 00; O. M. Avery, Representative, $252 60; T. Hannah, Representative, $165 00; H. J. Seward, Representative, $225 00; N. T. Scott, Representative, $149 00; J. L. Campbell, Representative, $175 00; Moses Hewett, Representative, $173 00; W. T. Duval, Representative, $245 00; B. F. Allen, Representative, $145 00; C. T. Jenkins, Representative, $211 80; Sam. C. Craft, Representative, $225 00; Thomas Y. Henry, Representative, $150 00; W. H. Gee, Representative, $149 80; Joseph Price, Representative, $167 00; L. Andreu, Representative, $187 00; I. V. Garnie, Representative, $181 00; A. J. Polhill, Representative, $160 00; T. J. W. Higginbotham, Representative, $185 00; J. Y. Jones, Representative, $151 00; Edward M. Mettauer, Representative, $149 00; J. N. Foy, Representative, $195 00; Henry Overstreet, Representative, $225 00; J. W. Price, Representative, $187 00; W. H. Arendell, Representative, $151 00; J. J. Williams, Representative, $145 00; J. S. Rust, Representative, $145 00; J. P. Atkins, Representative, $170 00; David Mizell, Representative, $225 00; Archibald Campbell, Representative, $157 00; Thomas B. Barefoot, Clerk House of Representatives, $180 00; W. F. Bynum, Assistant Clerk, $183 00; Thomas Williams, Engrossing Clerk, $145 50; W. M. McIntosh, Enrolling Clerk, $145 00; F. M. Bunker, Recording Clerk, $150 00; G. W. Floyd, Sergeant-at-Arms, $147 50; J. W. Tompkins, Messenger, $155 50; A. B. Campbell, Doorkeeper, $151 00; Chaplains, $50 each.

Printing and publishing. For general printing and publishing, to be audited by the Comptroller,............................. $9,000 00

Printing of the Laws and Journals, to be audited by the Comptroller upon contract terms, in addition to the above,............................. 1,500 00

McDougald & Hobby, Stationery,................. 320 53

Stationary, &c. Geo. H. Meginniss, Stationery,.................... 54 82

E. Barnard, Quartermaster-General, Candles,....... 38 00

A. Hopkins & Co., Candles,	75	00
M. Lively, Candles,	51	00
Servant hire,	40	00
W. M. McIntosh, Envelopes,	23	00

Sec. 2. *Be it further enacted*, That the following sums be and are hereby appropriated for the fiscal year eighteen hundred and sixty-three, to-wit:

For salaries of public officers,	\$31,000	00
For Jurors and State Witnesses,	20,000	00
For criminal prosecutions and contingent expenses of Circuit Court,	20,000	00
For contingent expenses of Supreme Court,	2,000	00
For interest on State Debt,	10,000	00
For maintenance of Lunatics,	10,000	00
For residence of the Governor,	500	00
For Post Mortem examinations,	400	00
For contingent fund,	20,000	00
For military purposes, in addition to the balance on hand,	10,000	00
For clerk hire for Executive Department,	1,000	00
For repairs and whitewashing the Capitol, to be audited by the Comptroller,	2,000	00
For the purpose of procuring Stationery for the use of the government, to be bought by the Comptroller, and Candles for the General Assembly,	500	00

Passed the Senate December 13, 1862. Passed the House of Representatives December 13, 1862. Approved by the Governor December 15, 1862.

RESOLUTIONS.

[No. 1.]

' RESOLUTION suspending the sale of Public Lands.

Be it resolved by the Senate and House of Representatives of the State of Florida in General Assembly convened, That the Register of Public Lands be and he is hereby instructed not to offer for sale or allow any public land to be entered until he receives further instructions from said General Assembly.

And be it further resolved, That he inform his sub-agents of the same, and that they govern themselves accordingly.

Passed the House of Representatives November 24, 1862. Passed the Senate November 24, 1862. Approved by the Governor November 26, 1862.

[No. 2.]

RESOLUTION of thanks to Florida Troops.

Resolved, unanimously, by the Senate and House of Representatives of the State of Florida in General Assembly convened, That the thanks of this General Assembly are eminently due, and are hereby tendered, to the Florida soldiers, officers and privates in the Confederate army, for the patriotic gallantry with which they responded to the call of their country, and for the characteristic courage and energy with which they have borne aloft the banner of their country on the bloody battlefields of Virginia and elsewhere, to the imperishable glory and honor of themselves and their State.

Resolved, unanimously, That this General Assembly begs, most sincerely, to mingle its sympathies with the relatives and friends of those who have fallen in the service of their country, whether in battle, amidst the clangor of arms, from wounds received in battle, from disease, or from accident.

Resolved, unanimously, That the children who have been, and may hereafter be made orphans by the fall of their fathers in defending their country against the invasion and devastation of a

1862.

relentless and cruel enemy, are pre-eminently the children of the State, and it is the duty of the constituted authorities to provide, as far as practicable, for their sustenance and education, and for training them up in such way that the State, in future years, " when asked for her jewels, may point to her sons," the offspring of fathers who fell gallantly defending the liberties of their country.

Resolved, unanimously, That his Excellency the Governor is hereby requested to cause a copy of these resolutions to be transmitted to officers commanding regiments, battalions and companies of Florida troops, with a request that they be communicated to their respective commands.

Passed the Senate November 25, 1862. Passed the House of Representatives November 25, 1862. Approved by the Governor November 28, 1862.

[No. 3.]

RESOLUTION authorizing the Governor to appoint Commissioners in relation to the Boundary Line between this State and the State of Georgia.

Resolved by the Senate and House of Representatives of the State of Florida in General Assembly convened, That the Governor be and he is hereby authorized to appoint two Commissioners to confer with similar Commissioners appointed by the State of Georgia in relation to the Boundary Line between the States of Georgia and Florida, and to make an adjustment and settlement of matters in controversy between the two States relative to said Boundary Line.

Be it further Resolved, That the said Commissioners shall report their proceedings under these resolutions to the Governor, who shall submit them to this General Assembly for their final action in relation to the Boundary Line between the States of Georgia and Florida.

Commissioners shall report.

Passed the House of Representatives November 28, 1862. Passed the Senate November 28, 1862. Approved by the Governor December 1, 1862.

[No. 4.]

RESOLUTION relative to Mails.

Be it resolved by the Senate and House of Representatives of the State of Florida in General Assembly convened, That the

LAWS OF FLORIDA.

Postmaster General of the Confederate States of America be and he is hereby requested to rescind his order dated February 27, 1862, and restore mail route No. 65 to three times per week, instead of once per week, as the said order now has it.

1862.

Mail route No. 65.

Passed the Senate November 24, 1862. Passed the House of Representatives November 25, 1862. Approved by the Governor December 2, 1862.

[No. 5.]

JOINT RESOLUTION in relation to sending the carpets at the Capitol for the use of the troops from this State.

Resolved by the Senate and House of Representatives of the State of Florida in General Assembly convened, That the Governor be, and he is hereby authorized to send to the proper Confederate officer carpets used at the Capitol which may be of service to the troops now in service from this State.

Passed the Senate November 29, 1862. Passed the House of Representatives December 1, 1862. Approved by the Governor December 4, 1862.

[No. 6.]

JOINT RESOLUTION to facilitate the procurement of cotton and wool cards by the citizens of this State.

Resolved by the Senate and House of Representatives of the State of Florida in General Assembly convened, That the sum of twenty thousand dollars is hereby appropriated and placed at the disposal of the Governor of the State for the purpose of purchasing and importing from abroad a quantity of Cotton and Wool Cards sufficient to supply the present necessity of the people of the State; the Governor shall cause said Cards to be distributed to the poor in each county in the State gratis and without charge; *Provided, however,* that if a surplus of said Cards remain after supplying the poor, the Governor shall cause the same to be sold at a price sufficient to remunerate the State for the number so disposed of by sale.

Appropriation.

Distribution of cards.

Passed the House of Representatives November 25, 1862. Passed the Senate December 5, 1862. Approved by the Governor December 8, 1862.

9

[No. 7.]

RESOLUTION to defray the burial expenses of Hon. A. Campbell, deceased.

Resolved by the Senate and House of Representatives of the State of Florida in General Assembly convened, That the Comptroller of Public Accounts be and he is hereby authorized to audit the bills of A. Hopkins & Co., for the amount of $10.25, Thos. Rawls for $15, and P. B. Brokaw for $30, and issue his Warrant for their order to the State Treasurer for the same, to be paid out of any money not otherwise appropriated.

Comptroller to audit account.

Passed the House of Representatives December 4, 1862. Passed the Senate December 5, 1862. Approved by the Governor December 8, 1862.

[No. 8.]

RESOLUTION authorizing the Governor to employ a Messenger.

Resolved by the Senate and House of Representatives of the State of Florida in General Assembly convened, That the Governor be and he is hereby authorized to employ a Messenger at the Capitol for and during the ensuing year; and he is hereby requested to employ as such Messenger, Richard E. Frier, who became disabled while in the military service of the State by the accidental discharge of a piece of ordnance.

Messenger.

Passed the Senate December 8, 1862. Passed the House of Representatives December 8, 1862. Approved by the Governor December 9, 1862.

[No. 9.]

RESOLUTION relating to the illegal sales of public lands in the Suwannee Circuit.

Resolved by the Senate and House of Representatives of the State of Florida in General Assembly convened, That where any person or persons have entered lands in the Suwannee Circuit, in the absence of the Receiver, from any person acting as agent or deputy of said Receiver, such person or persons shall not receive patents therefor from this State.

Patents shall not be issued.

Be it further Resolved, That the Register of Public Lands is hereby instructed to refund the purchase money to such illegal purchasers.

Passed the Senate December 5, 1862. Passed the House of Representatives December 8, 1862. Approved by the Governor December 10, 1862.

[No. 10.]

RESOLUTION requesting the Governor to secure the payment of customs on Railroad Iron due at the date of the secession of the State.

Be it resolved by the Senate and House of Representatives of the State of Florida in General Assembly convened, That the Governor he requested to take steps to secure the payment of the sums due, if any, for customs on Railroad Iron at the time of the secession of this State from the United States.

Governor shall take steps to secure payment.

Passed the House of Representatives December 6, 1862. Passed the Senate December 8, 1862. Approved by the Governor December 10, 1862.

[No. 11.]

RESOLUTION for the relief of the Hon. T. T. Long.

WHEREAS, the Clerk of the Circuit Court for Lafayette county has reported to the Comptroller of the State a failure on the part of the presiding Judge to hold the Fall Term of said Court ; and whereas, it appears that the said Judge had good and sufficient reasons for failing to hold said Court:

Preamble.

Be it resolved by the Senate and House of Representatives of the State of Florida in General Assembly convened, That the Hon. T. T. Long be relieved from the payment of the fine imposed by law, viz: ($100,) one hundred dollars, and that the Comptroller of the State be notified to this effect.

Fine remitted.

Passed the House of Representatives Dec. 6, 1862. Passed the Senate Dec. 8, 1862. Approved by the Governor Dec. 10, 1862.

[No. 12.]

RESOLUTION in relation to deceased Soldiers.

Be it resolved by the Senate and House of Representatives of the State of Florida in General Assembly convened, That it

1862.

I stry of names of deceased soldiers.

shall be the duty of the Governor of this State, as soon as practicable, to cause to be registered in alphabetical order, in a book to be used exclusively for that purpose, the names of all officers and soldiers killed in battle, or mustered into service, from the State of Florida during the present war, who may have been killed in battle or otherwise lost their lives whilst in the military service of their country.

Manner of registration.

Be it further resolved, That said registration shall state the county in which the deceased resided when he entered the service, the date of his enlistment and the term for which he enlisted, whether said service was State or Confederate, and the company to which he belonged, the time and place at which he lost his life, &c.

Title of book of registration.

Be it further resolved, That said book shall be styled "The Book of Honor," and shall be deposited in the office of the Secretary of State, there to remain subject to the inspection of the public, as a memorial of the patriotism and gallantry of our soldiers.

Passed the Senate November 20, 1862. Passed the House of Representatives December 9, 1862. Approved by the Governor December 10, 1862.

[No. 13.]

RESOLUTION relating to Salt.

Citizens of other States making salt in Florida.

Be it resolved by the Senate and House of Representatives of the State of Florida in General Assembly convened, That we cordially extend the privilege to our sister Confederate States of manufacturing Salt upon the coast of this State.

Be it further resolved, That the Governor of this State send a copy of these resolutions to the Governors of each of the Confederate States.

Passed the Senate December 6th, 1862. Passed the House of Representatives December 8th, 1862. Approved by the Governor December 10th, 1862.

[No. 14.]

JOINT RESOLUTION in relation to Public Lands in West Florida.

Be it resolved by the Senate and House of Representatives of the State of Florida in General Assembly convened, That the

Register of Public Lands shall cause copies of the maps of the lands in Calhoun and Jackson counties, and that the same be made applicable to the county of Washington, to be made, setting forth thereon those lands that are subject to entry and such as have been entered, with the price thereof, and said maps shall be sent by the Register to the Clerks of the Circuit Court of said counties, and shall be at all times subject to the inspection of the citizens of the State.

Register to make furnish maps.

Be it further resolved, That the citizens of West Florida may enter such lands as are by law authorized at Tallahassee, or at the office of the Receiver of the West, at their option.

Entry of lands.

Passed the Senate December 5, 1862. Passed the House of Representatives December 8, 1862. Approved by the Governor, December 10, 1862.

[No. 15.]

RESOLUTION relative to the Hospital at Richmond, Virginia.

Resolved by the Senate and House of Representatives of the State of Florida in General Assembly convened, That the application of three thousand five hundred dollars from the Treasury of the State, by his Excellency the Governor, to the use of the Florida Hospital in the city of Richmond, Virginia, meets the unqualified approbation of this General Assembly.

Application of funds approved.

Resolved further, That the Comptroller be required to audit and allow the same.

Appropriation.

Passed the Senate December 9, 1862. Passed the House of Representatives December 9, 1862. Approved by the Governor December 11, 1862.

[No. 16.]

RESOLUTION relative to Seals for the Judges of Probate of the counties of Levy and Sumter, and all other counties needing Seals.

Be it resolved by the Senate and House of Representatives of the State of Florida in General Assembly convened, That the Secretary of State be and he is hereby authorized and required to provide and furnish Seals of office to the Judges of Probate of the counties of Levy and Sumter and all other counties in this State requiring seals, in the same manner as is now provided for the Clerks of the Circuit Courts, the expense of providing said

Secretary of State to furnish seals.

Seals to be paid out of any money in the Treasury not otherwise appropriated.

Passed the House of Representatives December 8, 1862. Passed the Senate December 9, 1862. Approved by the Governor December 11, 1862.

[No. 17.]

RESOLUTION in relation to the present War.

Preamble.

WHEREAS, The State of Georgia has, in a spirit of fraternal sympathy, pledged herself by resolutions solemnly adopted by her Legislature to co-operate with her sister States of the Confederacy in the impending struggle for our lives and liberties, and to this end to contribute all the means at her command to the support of the common cause. Therefore,

Be it resolved by the Senate and House of Representatives of the State of Florida in General Assembly convened, That it is the sense of this Legislature that Florida, one of the first States to secede from the old Union, will be one of the last to lay down its arms, and in the impending struggle will stand by her sister States to the last man and the last musket, until peace is established on the basis of a separate nationality and the independence of the Confederate States is unconditionally acknowledged by the United States.

Be it further resolved, That a copy of said report and resolution be transmitted to the President of the Confederate States, and also to the Governors of each State, and to the Congress of the Confederate States.

Passed the House of Representatives Dec. 9, 1862. Passed the Senate Dec. 9, 1862. Approved by the Governor Dec. 11, 1862.

[No. 18.]

RESOLUTION relative to persons holding office in the State of Florida under the Confederate Government subject to the Conscript Act.

Be it resolved by the Senate and House of Representatives of the State of Florida in General Assembly convened, That our Representatives in Congress be and they are hereby instructed to use their influence with the proper department at Richmond to carry the following resolution into effect, viz:

Be it resolved, That all persons holding office in the State of Florida under the Confederate Government, subject to the military service under the Conscript Act, be removed and their places filled with persons not subject to the military service under said Conscript Act.

Resolution.

Passed the House of Representatives December 8, 1862. Passed the Senate December 10, 1862. Approved by the Governor December 12, 1862.

[No. 19.]

RESOLUTION relative to the Public Lands in Clay county.

Be it resolved by the Senate and House of Representatives of the State of Florida in General Assembly convened, That the Register of Public Lands be and he is hereby required to make out and transmit to the Clerk of the Circuit Court of Clay county township plats of all the lands in said county, designating thereon what lands have been entered, and what lands belong to the School, Seminary and Internal Improvement Funds, and the price of each tract, and also to furnish a list showing the dates of all entries and the names of purchasers of each tract of land.

Register to furnish maps and list of lands.

Passed the House of Representatives December 10, 1862. Passed the Senate December 11, 1862. Approved by the Governor December 13, 1862.

[No. 20.]

RESOLUTION requesting the President to allow persons in this State liable to conscription until 15th March, 1863, to volunteer in the Confederate service for the defence of the State.

WHEREAS, the citizens of the State of Florida, capable of bearing arms, have enlisted in the service of the Confederate States to so great an extent as to leave but few at home for the protection of the women and children of the State and the control of the slaves: *And whereas,* the number of slaves and the quantity of provisions, cotton and tobacco in the State, left thereby comparatively unprotected, by reason of the small number of troops serving in Florida, the proximity of the coast to the rich planting regions, and the accessibility of the country, by means

Preamble.

of the rivers St. Johns and Apalachicola, render the State an inviting field for invasion by the enemy: *And whereas*, a successful invasion by the enemy would be attended by most disastrous results to the country at large in the loss of a large number of slaves and a vast quantity of provisions, and in the evil of having one entire population thrown for support on the already burthened resources of other parts of the Confederacy, and in addition thereto, the State would become a rendezvous for fugitive slaves from Alabama and Georgia; therefore,

Be it resolved by the Senate and House of Representatives of the State of Florida in General Assembly convened, That the President of the Confederate States be and he is hereby requested to exempt all citizens of the State of Florida from conscription who shall, by volunteer enlistment, enter the service of the Confederate States by the 15th day of March, 1863, to be mustered into said service expressly for the defence of the State.

President requested to exempt citizens from conscription.

Passed the House of Representatives December 11, 1862. Passed the Senate December 12, 1862. Approved by the Governor December 13, 1862.

[No. 21.]

RESOLUTION authorizing the Treasurer to receive all genuine Confederate Notes of the Hoyer & Ludwig issue.

Be it resolved by the Senate and House of Representatives of the State of Florida in General Assembly convened, That the Treasurer of the State of Florida be and he is hereby authorized to receive from the Tax Collectors of the State, all genuine Confederate notes of the Hoyer & Ludwig issue, and to receive them for all Revenue due the State of Florida, and to have them exchanged so as to meet the arrangement as required; *Provided, however*, that the Treasurer shall only receive the notes of that issue which have been collected up to this time by the Tax Assessors and Collectors.

Proviso.

Passed the House of Representatives December 11, 1862. Passed the Senate December 13, 1862. Approved December 15, 1862.

[No. 22.]

RESOLUTION requiring information to be furnished by the Internal Improvement Board, with regard to the management of certain Railroads.

Resolved by the Senate and House of Representatives of the State of Florida in General Assembly convened, That the Board of Internal Improvement be and are hereby required to obtain from the Railroad Companies whose roads have been constructed or are in course of construction on routes indicated in the fourth section of the Act to provide for and encourage a liberal system of Internal Improvements, a statement showing the number of miles of road completed on the first day of January, 1863, a statement of work done on the uncompleted part, the number of acres of land reserved for each road under the Land Grants, the amount of Bonds endorsed by the Trustees of the Internal Improvement Fund, the number of said Bonds held by the Company, the number issued, to whom and on what account, the actual al cost per mile of the road, the amount of rolling stock and its cost, the amount in cash paid from the Internal Improvement Fund on the Interest Account of each road, the amount invested by the Internal Improvement Board in the Bonds of each road, the amount due by said Companies for interest remaining unpaid on said 1st January, 1863, the amount of private subscription to the stock of each Company, the amount received by each Company on account of private subscription, either in cash or notes, stating the amount of each, the amount of county subscriptions and the amount received either in cash, bonds or notes, stating the amount of each and the county subscribing.

Resolved, 2d, That the said Board be and they are hereby required to embrace in said statement any other facts, which in their judgment may be necessary to enable the General Assembly at their next session to form an accurate idea of the condition and management of the Railroad Companies above referred to.

Resolved, 3d, That the Governor be and he is hereby requested to obtain copies of the reports of all the Railroad Companies in this State from the commencement of the work on said roads, and place them in charge of the Secretary of State.

Resolved, 4th, That a copy of the statement above required, and a copy of each of the annual reports of the various companies, shall be laid before the General Assembly at its next meeting.

Passed the House of Representatives December 13, 1862. Passed the Senate December 13, 1862. Approved by the Governor December 15, 1862.

10

[No. 23.]

RESOLUTION in relation to compensation to Messrs. Papy and Banks.

Compensation of Commissioners.

Resolved by the Senate and House of Representatives of the State of Florida in General Assembly convened, That the Comptroller be required to issue his warrants in favor of the Hon. M. D. Papy and the Hon. James Banks for fifty dollars each as compensation for their services as Commissioners on the subject of boundary, and the Treasurer be authorized and required to pay the same.

Passed the Senate December 11, 1862. Passed the House of Representatives Dec. 12, 1862. Approved by the Governor Dec. 15, 1862.

[No. 24.]

RESOLUTION to appoint a Chaplain for the Florida Hospital at Richmond.

Governor to appoint Chaplain.

Resolved by the Senate and House of Representatives of the State of Florida in General Assembly convened, That the Governor is hereby authorized to appoint a Chaplain for the Florida Hospital at Richmond, Virginia, and shall cause said Chaplain to be paid a reasonable compensation for his services.

Passed the House of Representatives December 13, 1862. Passed the Senate December 13, 1862. Approved by the Governor December 15, 1862.

[No. 25.]

RESOLUTION requiring plats of the Public Lands to be furnished the various counties.

Register to make and furnish plats, &c.

Be it resolved by the Senate and House of Representatives of the State of Florida in General Assembly convened, That the Register of Public Lands be and he is hereby required to make and transmit to the Clerks of the Circuit Courts of all the counties in this State that may make application for such plats, as soon as practicable, township plats of all the lands in said county, designating thereon what lands have been entered and what lands belong to the School, Seminary and Internal Improvement Funds, and the price of each tract, and also to furnish a list showing the

dates of all entries and the names of purchasers of each tract of
land.

Be it further resolved, That the Clerk of the Circuit Court
shall keep them open for the examination of all who may desire.

Clerk of Circuit Court.

Be it further resolved, That the Register employ such clerks
as may be necessary to carry out these resolutions.

Passed the House of Representatives December 12, 1862. Passed the Senate
December 13, 1862. Approved by the Governor December 15, 1862.

[No. 26.]

RESOLUTION in relation to the Secretary of State.

WHEREAS, the present incumbent of the office of Secretary of
State of this State holds a commission in the military service
of the Confederate States: AND WHEREAS, there is a diversity
of opinion on the subject as to whether any commissioned officer of this State can, under our constitution, consistently hold
a Commission at the same time in the military service of the
Confederate States;

Preamble.

*Therefore be it Resolved by the Senate and House of Repre-
sentatives of the State of Florida in General Assembly convened,*
That the Attorney General be and he is hereby required to give
his opinion on the subject in writing as early as practicable to
this General Assembly.

Opinion of At-
torney General
required.

Passed the House of Representatives December 13, 1862. Passed the Senate
December 13, 1862. Approved by the Governor December 15, 1862.

[No. 27.]

RESOLUTION relative to the Books and Accounts of the Comptroller and
Treasurer.

*Resolved by the Senate and House of Representatives of the
State of Florida in General Assembly convened,* That a joint
committee, consisting of three members of the Senate and a like
number of the House of Representatives, shall be appointed by
the presiding officers of the Senate and House, whose duty it
shall be to examine the books, accounts and other matters of the
Comptroller and Treasurer's offices, which, in their opinion, ne-

Committee ap-
pointed to ex-
amine books of
Comptroller &
Treasurer.

1862.

cessarily appertain to the proper understanding of such books and accounts, and that it shall be the duty of said joint committee, or a majority of the same, to meet at the Capitol on the first Monday of November next, and shall sit from day to day until their labors are closed and a report of their examination is made, which said report shall be laid before the General Assembly at its next session, and the said committee shall be entitled to receive the same per diem as is now provided by law for members of the General Assembly.

Passed the House of Representatives December 12, 1862. Passed the Senate December 13, 1862. Approved by the Governor December 15, 1862.

[No. 28.]

RESOLUTION to allow pay, per diem and mileage to the legal representatives of the Hon. Archibald Campbell, deceased, late of Liberty county, Florida.

Be it Resolved by the Senate and House of Representatives of the State of Florida in General Assembly convened, That per diem, pay and mileage for this Session of the General Assembly be paid to the legal representatives of the Hon. Archibald Campbell, deceased, late a member of this Assembly from Liberty county in said State.

Passed the House of Representatives December 12, 1862. Passed the Senate December 12, 1862. Approved by the Governor December 15, 1862.

[No. 29.]

RESOLUTION to provide for furnishing Receivers with township plats in lieu of those that may be lost or destroyed.

Be it Resolved by the Senate and House of Representatives of the State of Florida in General Assembly convened, That whenever the Township plats of Public Lands in any of the Receiver's offices shall be lost or destroyed, it shall be the duty of the Register of Public Lands to furnish new plats in lieu thereof in accordance with the first and second Sections of "An act relative to the Public Lands of the State of Florida, approved December 17, 1861."

Register of Public Lands to furnish new plats.

Passed the House of Representatives December 11, 1862. Passed the Senate December 12, 1862. Approved by the Governor December 15, 1862.

[No. 30.]

JOINT RESOLUTION for organizing the Salt-makers upon the coast of Florida for their own and the public defence.

Be it resolved by the Senate and House of Representatives of the State of Florida in General Assembly convened, That citizens of this State, non-residents and persons not citizens of the State, engaged in making salt on the coast of this State, shall be organized under officers to be appointed by the Governor in a military capacity for their joint protection and defence against the enemy, under suitable regulations as to the discipline, number of arms, &c., to be furnished by the Governor.

Salt makers to organize.

Governor to appoint officers and furnish arms.

Be it further Resolved, That the Governor shall appoint three officers, with the rank of first Lieutenant, to command the said organization, whose duty it shall be to enrol, under such rules and regulations as the Governor may prescribe, the said persons for military duty, to see that their arms are secured and that they are in condition for service when the occasion arises, and when called upon by an apprehended invasion of the enemy, and when called into service and while acting as such they are hereby made subject to the rules and articles of war.

Officers to be appointed and their duties.

In case of invasion.

Be it further resolved, That any person refusing to enter such organization for, and during the time he may be on the coast for the purpose of making salt, shall be prohibited from doing so, and the officer in command shall enforce this provision: *Provided, however,* that this clause shall not prevent persons unable to bear arms from manufacturing salt upon our coast.

Persons refusing to enter organization.

Proviso.

Be it further resolved, That the salt-makers so organized shall have no claim against the State of Florida for the services they may render agreeably to this resolution.

Salt makers shall serve without pay.

Passed the Senate December 11, 1862. Passed the House of Representatives December 12, 1862. Approved by the Governor December 15, 1862.

[No. 31.]

JOINT RESOLUTION In relation to copies of acts to be distributed among the soldiers.

Resolved by the Senate and House of Representatives of the State of Florida in General Assembly convened, That the Governor is hereby authorized to have one thousand copies printed of the "act to aid the families of soldiers that require assistance," and one thousand copies printed of the "resolution relating to the Roll of Honor," passed at this session. and that he causes the same to be distributed among the soldiers from the State of Florida.

Passed the Senate December 11, 1862.   Passed the House of Representatives December 13, 1862.   Approved by the Governor December 15, 1862.

[No. 32.]

RESOLUTION in relation to copying the laws.

Be it resolved by the Senate and House of Representatives of the State of Florida in General Assembly convened, That the Governor be and he is hereby authorized to employ a suitable person to copy the laws passed at this session of the General Assembly, and the sum of one hundred and twenty-five dollars is hereby appropriated for said service.

Passed the Senate December 8, 1862.   Passed the House of Representatives December 11, 1862.   Approved by the Governor December 15, 1862.

[No. 33.]

RESOLUTIONS to guarantee by the States the debt of the Confederate Government.

Preamble.

WHEREAS, the Government of the Confederate States is involved in a war for the independence of each of the States of the Confederacy as well as for its own existence: *And whereas,* the destiny of each State of the Confederacy is indissolubly connected with that of the Confederate Government: *And whereas,* also, the Confederate Government cannot successfully prosecute the war to a speedy and honorable peace without ample means and credit;

Resolved, therefore, by the Senate and House of Representatives of the State of Florida in General Assembly convened,

Concurrence with the General Assembly of the State of Alabama.

That this General Assembly concurs in opinion with the General Assembly of the State of Alabama, that it is the duty of each State of the Confederacy, for the purpose of sustaining the credit of the Confederate Government, to guarantee the debt of that Government in proportion to its representation in the Congress of that Government.

Guarantee of Confederate debt.

Resolved further, That the State of Florida hereby accepts the proposition of the State of Alabama to guarantee said debt on said basis, provided each of the said States shall accept the proposition and adopt suitable legislation to carry it into effect, and 'that these resolutions shall stand as the guaranty of this State of the aforesaid proportion of the debt of said Confederate Government.

Resolved further, That His Excellency be and he is hereby requested to transmit a copy of these resolutions to the Governor of each State of the Confederacy and to the President of the Confederate Government.

Governor to transmit copies of resolutions.

Passed the Senate December 13, 1862. Passed the House of Representatives December 15, 1862. Approved by the Governor December 15, 1862.

[No. 34.]

JOINT RESOLUTION relative to the completion of the Pensacola & Georgia Railroad to the Apalachicola river.

WHEREAS, the early completion of the Pensacola & Georgia Railroad to the Apalachicola river, thereby bringing into immediate connection the different portions of the country comprehended in the district over which the command of Brigadier General Cobb extends, is, in the opinion of this General Assembly, a military necessity, which should not be overlooked by the State and Confederate Government: And, whereas, the completion of said Road to the Apalachicola river will not only greatly facilitate the efforts of the Commanding General defending the country assigned to his command, but will likewise aid in the defence of East Florida, by furnishing the means for the speedy transmission of supplies which may be drawn from upper Georgia, or through Columbus in this State, and will likewise afford an easy means to transfer to points in other States the abundant produce of our State, so needful for the support of our armies; therefore,

Preamble.

Be it resolved by the Senate and House of Representatives of the State of Florida in General Assembly convened, That the Governor be and he is hereby authorized and requested to urge upon the Confederate Government the great importance of completing, at an early day, the Pensacola and Georgia Railroad to Apalachicola River, and to obtain any aid the Confederate Government may be enabled to render in procuring the iron rail, or otherwise with a view to the speedy accomplishment of so important an object: *Provided,* that in the construction of said railroad, none of the iron shall be removed on any of the railroads now completed in the State of Florida.

Passed the Senate December 12, 1862. Passed the House of Representatives December 13, 1862. Approved by the Governor December 15, 1862.

INDEX

TO THE

ACTS AND RESOLUTIONS

OF THE

First Session of the Twelfth General Assembly.